CECIL BEATON
The Royal Portraits
ROY STRONG

SIMON AND SCHUSTER

NEW YORK   LONDON   TORONTO   SYDNEY   TOKYO

Eileen Joyce Hose

devoted secretary to Sir Cecil Beaton

in memoriam

Endpapers:
the detail from Jean Honoré Fragonard's *Girl on a Swing* which
Beaton used as a backdrop for many royal photographs in the 1930s
and 1940s.
Frontispiece:
a detail from *The Lord Mayor's River Procession, 1844*, an engraving by
Edward Goodall after David Roberts. This view of Westminster
Abbey from the river provided one of the backdrops for Beaton's
Coronation photographs of 1953.

Published by Simon and Schuster
A Division of Simon & Schuster Inc.
Simon & Schuster Building
Rockefeller Center
1230 Avenue of the Americas
New York, New York 10020

SIMON AND SCHUSTER and colophon are registered
trademarks of Simon & Schuster Inc.
Simultaneously published in Great Britain by Thames and Hudson Ltd.
Printed and bound in Japan by Dai Nippon

1   3   5   7   9   10   8   6   4   2

Library of Congress Cataloging in Publication Data

Strong, Roy C.
    Cecil Beaton: the royal portraits / Roy Strong.
        p.   cm.
    Bibliography: p.
    Includes index.
    ISBN 0-671-67033-6
    1. Windsor, House of—Portraits.   2. Great Britain—Kings and
rulers—Portraits.   3. Monarchy—Great Britain—History—20th
century—Pictorial works.   4. Photography—Portraits.   5. Beaton,
Cecil Walter Hardy, Sir, 1904–1980.   I. Title.
DA28.35.W54S76 1988
941.082'092'2—dc19
[B]   88-6744
                                                               CIP

CONTENTS

THE ROYAL HOUS

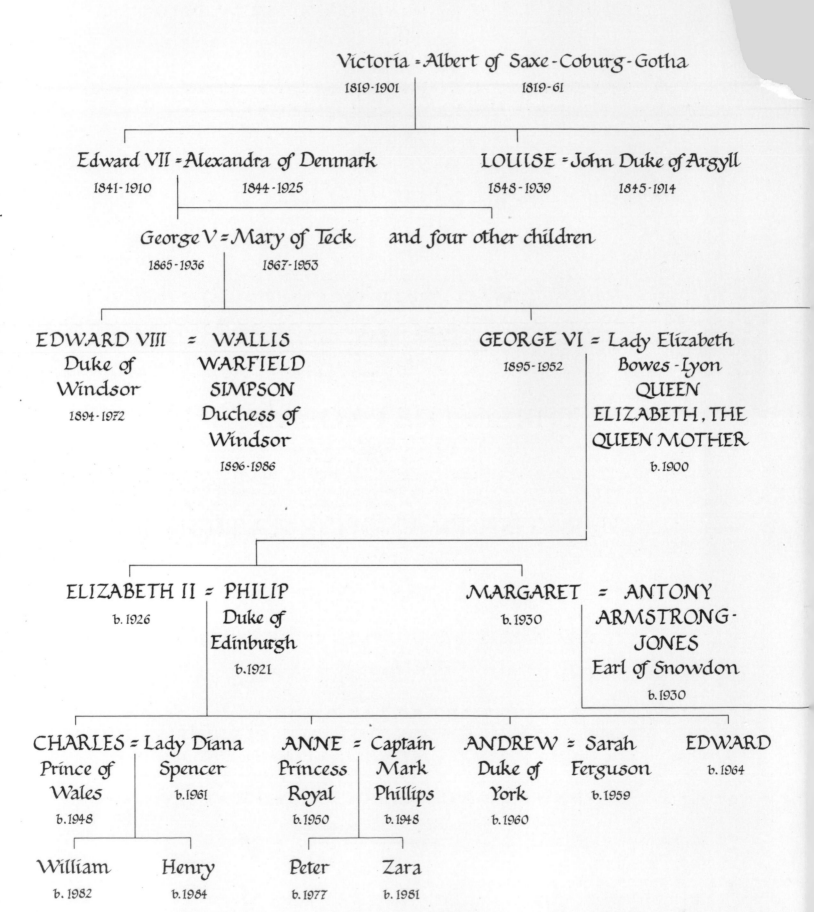

Victoria = Albert of Saxe-Coburg-Gotha
1819-1901 — 1819-61

Edward VII = Alexandra of Denmark
1841-1910 — 1844-1925

LOUISE = John Duke of Argyll
1848-1939 — 1845-1914

George V = Mary of Teck   and four other children
1865-1936 — 1867-1953

EDWARD VIII = WALLIS
Duke of   WARFIELD
Windsor   SIMPSON
1894-1972   Duchess of
Windsor
1896-1986

GEORGE VI = Lady Elizabeth
1895-1952   Bowes-Lyon
QUEEN
ELIZABETH, THE
QUEEN MOTHER
b.1900

ELIZABETH II = PHILIP
b.1926   Duke of
Edinburgh
b.1921

MARGARET = ANTONY
b.1930   ARMSTRONG-
JONES
Earl of Snowdon
b.1930

CHARLES = Lady Diana
Prince of   Spencer
Wales   b.1961
b.1948

ANNE = Captain
Princess   Mark
Royal   Phillips
b.1950   b.1948

ANDREW = Sarah
Duke of   Ferguson
York   b.1959
b.1960

EDWARD
b.1964

William   Henry
b.1982   b.1984

Peter   Zara
b.1977   b.1981

OF WINDSOR

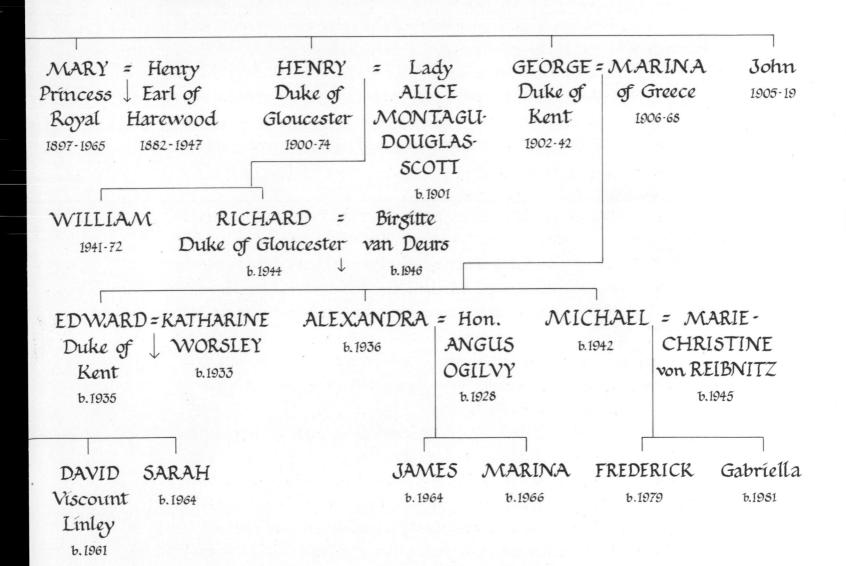

Helena = Christian of Schleswig-Holstein   and six other children
1846-1923 | 1831-1917

MARIE LOUISE
1872-1956

MARY = Henry   HENRY = Lady   GEORGE = MARINA   John
Princess ↓ Earl of   Duke of   ALICE   Duke of   of Greece   1905-19
Royal   Harewood   Gloucester   MONTAGU-   Kent   1906-68
1897-1965 1882-1947   1900-74   DOUGLAS-   1902-42
                                    SCOTT
                                    b.1901

WILLIAM   RICHARD = Birgitte
1941-72   Duke of Gloucester   van Deurs
            b.1944   ↓   b.1946

EDWARD = KATHARINE   ALEXANDRA = Hon.   MICHAEL = MARIE-
Duke of ↓ WORSLEY   b.1936   ANGUS   b.1942   CHRISTINE
Kent   b.1933   OGILVY   von REIBNITZ
b.1935   b.1928   b.1945

DAVID   SARAH   JAMES   MARINA   FREDERICK   Gabriella
Viscount   b.1964   b.1964   b.1966   b.1979   b.1981
Linley
b.1961

The names of Beaton's sitters are capitalized

THE ROMANTIC ROYALIST:

Cecil Beaton

AND THE IMAGE OF MONARCHY

CECIL BEATON'S CAREER AS ROYAL PHOTOGRAPHER SPANS ALMOST fifty years, from 1930 until 1979. In that period he photographed nearly thirty members of the House of Windsor, stretching from the children of King George V and Queen Mary to the children of Queen Elizabeth II and the Duke of Edinburgh. The archive of Beaton's royal photographs was bequeathed by his devoted secretary Eileen Hose to the Victoria and Albert Museum, London, in 1987. It contains the results of nearly seventy sittings: approximately 10,000 vintage prints and colour transparencies and about 8,000 negatives crammed into two filing cabinets.

The sheer quantity of this material is overwhelming. But it is also immensely exciting, for it opens a door into Beaton's mind as he fashioned the image of the Royal Family over nearly half a century, affecting the world's perception of the British monarchy in the process. A look through the folders enables us to see the photographer in action. Here are contact sheets on which his pen has marked which pictures should be enlarged and printed, often with scribbled instructions to the printer or retoucher. There are montages of the 'approved' pictures selected for publication by the sitters and guide prints to which all future copies had to be matched.

This pictorial material is supplemented by something unique and extraordinary – the vivid, witty accounts of the sittings which Beaton wrote in his diary. All the important sittings warranted an entry, often very extensive. Heavily edited versions of some appear in the six volumes of diaries published in Beaton's lifetime, and unedited extracts from the one hundred and forty-five volumes of manuscript diary now in the library of Beaton's old college, St

John's, Cambridge, are used by Hugo Vickers in his authorized biography. This is the first time that extracts describing the royal sittings have been used in full to provide a context for the photographs. In addition to the diary are the forty-five volumes of press cuttings which Eileen Hose gave to the Victoria and Albert Museum's Archive of Art and Design. They complete the story of the royal sittings, for in them are pasted the cuttings from every magazine or newspaper in which the pictures were reproduced.

It is in that global distribution of royal images that Beaton's importance lies. I can remember the surprise that greeted a suggestion I made in 1971 that Beaton should be given a knighthood (he received one the following year). When the secretary of the committee that made recommendations for honours asked me for my reasons, I replied that Beaton played a key role in restoring the image of the monarchy after the Abdication crisis of 1936. He − more than any other photographer − had re-created a powerful visual mythology for the Crown after Edward VIII's disastrous dabbling with modernism.

In a review of Beaton's retrospective exhibition at the National Portrait Gallery in 1968, the critic Keith Roberts acutely pointed out that 'Beaton is, I would have thought, an equivalent to Sir Joshua Reynolds in painting with sitters from every walk of life and an eclectic talent for borrowing visual ideas from a wide variety of sources. Like Reynolds (and, indeed, most professional portraitists), Mr Beaton grasped from the beginning that portraiture is not so much about likeness as about imagery.' Furthermore, Beaton was by virtue of talent and temperament the ideal man for the task the Royal Family set him. He was a romantic who idolized the pre-1914 world of the courts which had been swept away in a tide of war and revolution; for Beaton royalty should always be mysterious and heroic. He placed the whole range of his abilities in the service of the Crown, to flatter and idealize it by means of the camera's lens, surrounding the Royal Family with panoply, glamour and mystique, yet, at the same time, giving it an accessible human face more suited to a democratic age.

To me it is Beaton's profound sense of the historic past which sets his work apart and makes it unequalled in this century by any of the photographers that preceded or followed him. Indeed, it is no exaggeration to place his work alongside that of Holbein, Velazquez or Van Dyck, for it offers a similar heady combination of art and propaganda. For an article in *Vogue* in 1940, Beaton photomontaged one of his own romantic 1939 photographs of the Queen onto a series of reproductions of oil paintings of earlier British royalty, deliberately and accurately placing his work for the Royal Family in a direct line of descent from the court painters of the past. Beaton's portraits, therefore, played a crucial part in the creation of what recent historians have categorized as 'the invention of tradition'. They formed and still form a visual canon framing not only how we view the Crown but also how the Crown wished – and wishes – to be viewed. In spite of the flood of images of royalty on film and television and in newspapers and magazines, no historian or biographer can afford to ignore Beaton's status in the iconography of twentieth-century monarchy.

Photographer royal

To photograph the Royal Family represented the height of Beaton's almost limitless social ambitions, as one of the more curious entries in his early diaries reveals. This is an account of a visit in 1926 to a clairvoyant named Mrs Salisbury. At first she made fairly accurate predictions about many of his successes as a stage designer and as a figure in the public eye. Afterwards she said:

'"You'll have a lot to do with royalty."

This sounded so grand as to be utterly unbelievable. It sobered me up. Indeed, I began to wonder whether anything she said could possibly be true?' (*The Wandering Years*, p. 102).

Although Beaton was to have friendships of a kind with members of the Royal Family, any equality in such relationships was inevitably a mirage which, later in life, he came increasingly to recognize and resent. However famous and glamorous he had become, at root, as far as his royal sitters were concerned, he was just a photographer whose paid task was to take portraits circumscribed by regulations laid down by the Palace, which he also came to resent. This helps to explain the extraordinary candour and occasional acerbity of his diary entries describing the sittings.

What we witness, therefore, is a unique dialogue between an extremely complex, vain and uncertain man and representatives of a ruling family who possess all the certainty that a centuries-old monarchy must bring to its members. Beaton often felt that he was on the losing side of that dialogue, but the diaries reveal only his side of that story as he struggled with household officials and the brusquer members of the Royal Family, such as the Duke of Edinburgh, who clearly regarded him as a freak to be endured or even sent up. One of the few glimpses of the attitude of those facing his camera is a story about the late Duke of Gloucester who, when told in 1961 that he was to be photographed by Beaton, said 'that's the fella with the floppy hat, isn't it? Can't stand the man. Never stops talking in a funny voice. Bloody suspicious I think.' A message was sent via an equerry that His Royal Highness would *not* consent to being photographed peering through cascades of flowers.

Beaton's work for the Royal Family can be neatly divided into four periods. The first, leading up to World War II, covers his early infatuation with the monarchy, whose members were seen as both fashionable beauties and characters from a fairytale. The war was an interruption, and Beaton felt frustrated by the requirement to show the Royal Family as ordinary people involved in the common national effort. He was happier with the task of creating romantic images of the young Princesses Elizabeth and Margaret to cheer the country in the bleak 1940s. With the Queen's accession in 1952 he came into his own, producing portraits of a sumptuously regal glamour that has never been matched. Increasingly the lives of the Royal Family became remote from those of their subjects and a greater element of make-believe and pageantry entered into the monarchy, culminating in the medieval splendours of the 1953 Coronation ceremony, for which Beaton was the official photographer. However, both the Royal Family and Beaton were quick to respond to a change of public attitude in the 1960s, prompting a transformation in royal photography as complete as any scene change Beaton devised for the stage. The new image that the monarchy wished to project was relaxed and open, so out went the fairytale backdrops and many of the elaborate costumes; instead the Queen and her children were photographed against plain backgrounds, posing informally in their everyday clothes.

What did not change throughout, however, were the actual mechanics whereby a royal photograph was taken. Sittings were almost invariably triggered off by an event: a marriage, a birthday, an impending royal tour or a birth. The initiative lay with the sitter and the advisers, as also did the choice of photographer. Beaton's earliest work for the Royal Family was commissioned by members who were in some way artistic. The first was Princess Louise, the sculptress daughter of Queen Victoria, the second was Prince George, Duke of Kent, who shared with his mother, Queen Mary, a marked predilection for the arts and a fine sense of contemporary style in dress and interior decoration. Sitting for Beaton must have been quite daring in 1932–3 and it is perhaps significant that the resulting film-star-like portraits were never publicly issued, apart from one which appeared in American *Vogue*. Beaton wrote calculatingly of the Duke: 'he is definitely in my plan of campaign' (Diary, 30 January 1933). The Duke of Kent was very close to his eldest brother, Edward, Prince of Wales. Beaton had earlier photographed Wallis Simpson and indeed it was in her flat that he first encountered the Prince. The result of these connections was the commission to produce favourable pictures of her for the press in the summer of 1937 and then to take the wedding photographs.

What is more intriguing is how Beaton, who had so assiduously cultivated the Prince of Wales's smart set, managed to gain favour with what were in his own words the 'dull' Duke and Duchess of York, who ascended the throne as George VI and Queen Elizabeth after Edward VIII's abdication in 1936. The link seems to have been the Duchess of Kent's sister, Princess Paul of Yugoslavia, who stayed at Buckingham Palace in the summer of 1939, when Beaton photographed her. The ensuing summons to photograph the Queen is history, for it established a potent image where there had been none before. The rapport between photographer and sitter seems to have been instant and it lasted Beaton's lifetime. Queen Elizabeth was to be responsible for extending his work into the next generation of the Royal Family. It was at her suggestion that in 1948 he photographed Princess Elizabeth and the infant Prince Charles, a sitting so successful in its results that he was asked to photograph each of the Queen's children soon after their arrival. To the Queen Mother he seems also to have owed the commission to take the official photographs of the Coronation, despite the competition of the Duke of Edinburgh's protégé, Baron. Those loyalties did not descend to the third generation, of whom Prince Charles alone granted a sitting. In the case of the Duke and Duchess of Kent, the friendship was sustained by their children, especially Princess Alexandra, who continued to sit until shortly before Beaton had his stroke in 1974, when otherwise his position as royal photographer had slipped.

Apart from members of the Royal Family, Beaton had two major allies within the Palace. The first was Sir Martin (later Lord) Charteris, who was Private Secretary to the present Queen as Princess, and afterwards successively Assistant Secretary and Private Secretary to her until his retirement in 1972. The second was Patrick, 7th Lord Plunket, a close personal friend of the Queen. He was equerry to George VI from 1948 to 1952 and subsequently Deputy Master of the Household from 1954 to his death in 1975. Both these men were at the heart of the royal decision-making about monarchical style and public image. Both were sensitive about visual matters, not always a major ingredient in the personalities of courtiers and household officials. Lord Charteris is a sculptor. Lord Plunket's talents were of a more theatrical kind, for he was responsible for orchestrating the arrangements for formal occasions, from a state banquet to a ball at Windsor Castle. He combined the eye of a director in the theatre with that of an interior decorator. History alone will

---

The Queen at Buckingham Palace, 1955. She wears the sash of the Order of the Garter and a diamond and pearl diadem made for George IV. Overleaf: Left, Queen Elizabeth the Queen Mother in 1953, in front of a backdrop depicting Windsor Castle. Her jewels are the 'Indian' tiara and necklace made for Queen Victoria. Right, Princess Margaret in 1949, at the age of nineteen.

Prince Charles at Buckingham Palace in 1968, when he was nineteen.

evaluate the exact significance of these men in the evolution of the image of the Crown during this period, but there is no doubt that both were keenly aware of what Beaton could do for the monarchy in an age of mass media. They recognized the public hunger for pictures of the Royal Family and they realized the importance of supplying ones which reflected accurately what the monarchy represented. More to the point, they were also aware of the effectiveness of a good rather than an indifferent photograph.

It is easy to forget that at no point was Beaton ever the sole royal photographer. All the household officers, including in particular those in the Press Office, about which Beaton complained much, ensured that no single photographer had the monopoly. Throughout Beaton's long career the Royal Family sat for many other photographers, from Lisa Sheridan to Marcus Adams and, later, from Snowdon to Norman Parkinson. None of them, however, was to have such sustained patronage and none of them has produced such an important impact on the public.

A royal sitting

The diaries tell us a lot about the procedure that followed any summons to photograph. One fact emerges very definitely. There is nothing spontaneous about any royal photograph. A photographer was admitted only for a set period of time, which in the case of an event such as the Coronation or a wedding could be quite short for it was just one part of a long day of prolonged ceremonial. Whatever the circumstances, it meant that everything always had to be thought of and prepared in advance. Beaton would alight upon an idea and then work it out with the household officials, so that dress and location were decided upon before the actual encounter. In 1945, for example, before a sitting by Princess Elizabeth, he went to Buckingham Palace 'to see the Princess's dresses, which were hung up for display around the walls of her bedroom' (*Photobiography*, p. 144). Three years later Norman Hartnell specially made a crinoline of black velvet so that Beaton could photograph the Queen in the manner of the Victorian painter Winterhalter. In 1968 it was Martin Charteris who, prompted by Beaton's request for a simple outfit, suggested that the Queen wear a dark naval cape. There were, of course, suggestions on the Palace side, and a single sitting could involve several changes of dress involving both day and evening clothes as well as the ceremonial robes of the orders of chivalry such as the Garter and the Thistle.

Beaton had to work at enormous speed, for royal time was limited. Patrick Matthews, who was the *Vogue* studio manager for many years, and sometimes assisted Beaton, described to me the semi-military operation which any sitting entailed. Apart from the Kents, members of the Royal Family never visited the studio. Equipment had to be transported to the location. He remembers Beaton's use of a tray with four or six lights masked by layers of tissue paper which were adjusted to give a harder or softer light to the black and white pictures. Technically, he recalls, Beaton was not good but his eye was marvellous. Perhaps one might qualify that and say that Beaton may earlier in his career have been more proficient, but with the passing of time he went on to delegate such matters to his entourage. Technicians and assistants were employed only if they were capable of carrying out for him work recognizable unmistakably as 'Beaton'. During the 1930s his cameras changed. For his *Vogue* work, Condé Nast insisted that instead of the hand-held cameras he had worked with since boyhood he should use a 10 × 8 model fitted with a 12″ f/6.3 Kodak Commercial Ekbar which permitted marvellous detail. This was essential because the relatively crude half-tone reproduction processes used by magazines necessitated high-definition prints. Later, at the suggestion of his fellow *Vogue* photographer George Hoyningen-Huene, he bought a Rolleiflex camera for travel. During a sitting, the large camera with its 10 × 8 inch plates was set up for use but most shots were taken with a Rolleiflex. As many as a dozen of these were to hand ready loaded and an assistant would just feed him with a new one, saying 'black and white' or 'colour'.

The shots once taken, the film was sent on to be developed and printed elsewhere. Beaton was always to rely in his photography, as in his stage design, on a long series of assistants and technicians who carried out his vision, but the vision always remained his. In that lay his genius. That he relied on these people one knows from the poignant entry in his diary in 1955 on the death of Mr Herbert of Jeffrey & Boarder, and the folding of the firm on which he had relied for so long to print his pictures: 'now the struggle for good prints must continue, and quite possibly it will lead me into despair, frustration or taking pictures only with a big camera' (Diary, July 1955).

Retouching always arouses a frisson of excitement when royal photographs are involved. What is forgotten, however, is that it was the norm for all portrait photography until the 1960s. When the National Portrait Gallery's retrospective exhibition of his photographs was being planned in 1968, I remember Beaton sitting with a print of the Queen Mother and Prince Charles taken at the Coronation. He licked his finger and slowly rubbed off the retouching, saying: 'Now it can be done.' That remark summed up a profound shift towards a new realism in portrait photography. Until then retouching, both of the negative and of the final print, was the norm: wrinkles were obliterated, chin lines tidied up or waistlines reduced, just as in fashion photography. Problems arose only with early colour photographs, which could not be retouched, and it is interesting to compare the colour with the black and white prints to see the modifications. What is most striking is that the earliest record we have of a move to reduce retouching came not from the photographer but from the Queen Mother as early as 1950:

The most recent photographs I have taken of the Queen were to be used in connexion with the celebration of her fiftieth birthday; and once again Her Majesty consented to give up several hours to the sitting. After I sent about two dozen of the finished proofs to the Queen's Private Secretary, he telephoned to tell me that Her Majesty had seen the pictures, liked them extremely well, but considered I had been perhaps too kind. Her Majesty felt that, since she had battled her way through a number of years, she could not have come through completely unscathed. Would it be possible at this stage to take away the retouching? This is the first time that any of my sitters has suggested that the pictures were too flattering (*Photobiography*, p. 155).

There then followed the process of selection, one involving the sitter, household officials and other interested parties. Beaton used to submit up to thirty prints from which about ten would be chosen. These occupied the status of 'approved' royal portraits. None of the rejects could be issued although Beaton often thought his best photographs lurked amongst them. Sometimes he would get clearance to reproduce them years after the event, and many are reproduced in this book. In the case of the 'approved' pictures, some would be for immediate release on a date set by the press officer, others would be for bestowal privately by the sitter. In the case of the presentation of royal photographs, elaborate guidelines exist concerning the size of each signed photograph relative to the rank and office of the recipient.

Romance and reality

Until the mid-1950s Beaton made extensive use of artificial backgrounds, both painted and photographic. He loved the painted cloths that appeared in Victorian and Edwardian photographs and in some of his earliest fancy portraits there appear rather crudely painted rococo backdrops by himself. By the 1930s, however, he got others to execute cloths and he had discovered photographic blow-ups, then a rare and expensive commodity. The backgrounds begin in the 1930s with an enlargement in reverse of Fragonard's *Girl on a Swing* in the Wallace Collection but with the girl painted out, thus giving him the aureole of light with which he surrounded each sitter. This and the other backgrounds were not reserved solely for members of the Royal Family, but were used indiscriminately for any sitter. This Fragonard backdrop had a particularly long royal life, starting with the Duchess of Gloucester in 1938, moving on through the Duchess of Kent in the same year, the Queen in 1939, Princess Elizabeth in 1945 and finally the Duchess of Kent in 1949. Its creation must have been a reflection of the rococo revival of the 1930s. A second picture by Fragonard, the *Gardens of the Villa d'Este*, also in the Wallace Collection, similarly had a long life, appearing first in the wartime pictures of the two Princesses in 1942 and last glimpsed behind Princess Margaret in 1950. Both these backgrounds were deliberately used to make Beaton's portraits look like grand formal portraits of the eighteenth and nineteenth centuries. The allusion in both is arcadian and aristocratic with overtones of the *ancien régime*.

Photographic blow-ups were expensive, so that it is hardly surprising that his repertory was never a large one. They were carried out for him by a firm in Ealing. Beaton records in his diary that just before he went to photograph the Royal Family at Windsor in 1943, 'we started off ... in a Palace car and collected a new background (Velvet Breughel) in Ealing en route'. It is not possible to identify this particular blow-up but it may be one of the nondescript groups of trees whose source defies identification. Over others there is no problem: the grand false perspective arcade by Borromini in the Palazzo Spada in Rome, Roman ruins enlarged from an engraving by Francis Vivares after Pannini (Beaton wrongly referred to it always as his 'Piranesi') or a section of the background of a strange mannerist picture by Niccolò dell' Abbate in the National Gallery. The terminal date for the use of these backgrounds is the Coronation in 1953, when he deployed the groups before enlargements of two prints, one of the interior of Henry VII's Chapel and the other an early Victorian view of Westminster Abbey from the river. Their archaism, however, was appropriate to this spectacle lifted from an earlier age.

As well as the photographic blow-ups there were painted cloths. The first to be used in a royal photograph appears behind the Duchess of Kent in 1937 and shows ballet dancers in a sylvan woodland setting. Rex Whistler was responsible for the skating scene in the snow with a reclining river god in the foreground, which forms the somewhat incongruous background to pictures of Princesses Elizabeth and Margaret in 1945. The diaries shed no light on this

---

In the 1960s Beaton experimented with a variety of novel approaches to his royal sitters. Here he is shown in the process of photographing Princess Alexandra (see overleaf). This snapshot, by Beaton's assistant Geoffrey Sawyer, was published in 1968.

Beaton at work

The result of the sitting with Princess Alexandra
appears in a contact print (left). Princess Alexandra
also appears (with her family) in the elysian setting of
Richmond Park in 1966; Beaton is on the left of the
picture. The photographer himself took the self-
portrait below as he photographed Prince Charles in
1948.

The snapshot above, of Beaton with Princess
Alexandra in the 1950s, records one of the rare
occasions on which a royal sitter visited a studio.
Assistants snapped Beaton photographing
Princess Margaret at Clarence House in 1956
(right) and in the garden at Kensington Palace
in the 1960s (top right): Lord Snowdon is
lending professional assistance.

Behind the scenes

Royal portraits were often subjected to manipulation behind the scenes
before publication. This was usually at the photographer's instigation,
but occasionally the sitter intervened with specific requirements.
This 1937 portrait of the Duchess of Kent (above) is a complete
success in its own right, but the Duchess preferred the cropped
version on the left. Retouching was a matter that required
considerable tact. The 1956 study of the Queen Mother on
the right was improved by cropping and the airbrushing out
of distracting detail; extensive retouching of the portrait of
the Duke of Windsor in 1960 has converted the sixty-
six-year-old Duke into an image of his youthful self.
Even in 1937, Beaton recognized the difficulties in
producing photographs that 'will not be flattering
to him, accustomed to highly retouched
photographs taken many years ago'.

The world of Cecil Beaton

Beaton's work for the Royal Family can best be understood by being seen in the context of his career both as photographer of fashion and society and as designer for theatre and film. His idealization of royalty owed an incalculable debt to his highly glamorous presentation of Hollywood stars, his elegant fashion photography for Vogue and other magazines and his spectacular stage designs.

The use of mirrors is a recurrent theme in Beaton's work. The composition of this 1930 fashion photograph of Mariana Van Rensselaer in a Charles James hat (right) was redeployed in his portrait of the Duchess of Gloucester in 1961 (page 209).

Beaton's crisply elegant portraits of the Windsors and Kents in the 1930s are closely allied to his photography for fashion magazines, such as this study of Princess Karam Kapurthala in 1934 (above). When the Royal Family required a new image after the Abdication crisis, Beaton turned to the Edwardian revival that he was to pioneer on the stage: right, Isabel Jeans in Lady Windermere's Fan, 1945.

Film and stage provided ideals of male and female beauty that Beaton applied to the Royal Family. At the age of three he glimpsed a photograph of the musical comedy actress Lily Elsie: 'the beauty of it caused my heart to leap' he later wrote. Thereafter he collected pictures of her: this portrait (above, right) once belonged to him. Such images represented a photographic tradition that he transferred to his favourite royal beauties, such as Princess Alexandra. The photograph of Gary Cooper in 1931 (above) embodies the type of erotic masculinity with which Beaton endowed Prince George, Duke of Kent, and the Duke of Edinburgh.

Beaton's characteristic rococo neo-romanticism was successfully drawn on to help create a new look for the Royal Family in the 1930s. Arcadian, with wistful overtones of the ancien régime, it was first applied to society beauties and actresses of the 1930s, as in this portrait of Tilly Losch (right). The manner was first used for a royal sitter in the romantic photographs of the Duchess of Kent in 1938 (pages 76–77).

The images within the montage carry the following labels:

George V
A. S. Cope

Edward VII and Queen Alexandra—Barraud

Queen Henrietta Maria—Van Dyck

George III and his Family—Zoffany

The First May—Winterhalter

Princess Sophia—Reynolds

The Duchess of York
and the Princesses
Edmund Brock

Beaton's montage above uses one of his 1939 photographs of Queen Elizabeth to place his work in the great tradition of painted portraiture. Sir George Hayter's portrait of Queen Victoria in her Coronation robes (left) was an inspiration for Beaton's Coronation photographs (see page 108, for example). In 1948 he imitated Winterhalter's portrait of the Empress Eugénie in this photograph of the Queen (opposite, above), and his double portrait of Princesses Elizabeth and Margaret in 1942 (opposite, below) is based on one of Gainsborough's portraits of his daughters.

The fairy-tale effect of Beaton's romantic portraits is due in large part to his painted or photographic backdrops. Their use over the years gives a consistency and sense of tradition to his royal portraiture. Watteau's Pleasures of the Ball (above) forms an appropriate background for the nineteen-year-old Princess Margaret in 1949. One of Beaton's favourite backdrops was an enlarged and reversed detail from Fragonard's Girl on a Swing (opposite). It was first used to photograph the Duchess of Gloucester in 1938 (top left) and was re-used for several sitters, including the Queen a year later (bottom left) and Princess Elizabeth in 1945 (bottom right).

A make-believe world

'the fairy Queen in her
ponderous palace'

Beaton's inspired photographs of Queen Elizabeth in
Buckingham Palace in 1939 (above) brilliantly use
shafts of sunlight to transform the heavily ornate
interiors into an appropriate setting for the ethereal
figure. This use of natural light seems to have been
suggested to Beaton by a picture he much admired, Sir
John Lavery's portrait of George V and Queen
Mary with the Prince of Wales and the Princess
Royal at Buckingham Palace, painted in 1913.

strange choice of setting, but three years later they do provide a detailed account of how his 'Winterhalter' of the Queen was constructed. Martin Battersby, then working for him as an assistant in the theatre, painted the cloth – rather badly – copying it from the background of Winterhalter's famous 1853 full-length of the Empress Eugénie. Two years later there appears a final, far better, painted cloth to back photographs of the Queen Mother occasioned by her fiftieth birthday. This time it is a pastiche in the manner of Rex Whistler, a lyrical garden capriccio with fountains and a pavilion based on one in the gardens of Stowe. Beaton had terrible difficulty lighting nearly all these artificial backgrounds, particularly if they were to be for a full length. Time and again marvellous pictures are marred by folds and reflections in the cloths behind the sitter.

It is impossible to discuss these artificial backgrounds without mentioning their pendant prop of flowers. This formula was already a well established one by the time that Beaton came to take royal photographs in the 1930s: an artificial background before which the sitter stood or was seated, the sides and foreground built up and filled in with flowers. Beaton seized flowers or potted plants to hand in the room, or brought them in from the florist or his own garden in the country at Reddish, in Wiltshire. Flowers run as a leitmotif throughout his pictures. Even when the era of backcloths had gone he still returned to them as, for example, when he photographed the baby Prince Andrew amidst carnations, lilies of the valley and other spring flowers in 1960. Flowers were a very personal statement, almost a signature. Beaton loved them. His house in the country, I remember, was filled with vases of them even in winter; explosions of bloom ascended in the Gothic conservatory, each guest room had its bouquet and every mealtime was the occasion for a table display. When he travelled up by train from the country to London he carried boxes of blossoms for his house in Pelham Place – and no guest left Reddish in lilac time without armloads.

From the outset Beaton was unique in another way, for he was the first photographer to make extensive use of the architecture of the palaces and residences of members of the Royal Family. These, of course, are largely closed to the public so that their appearance in the background of his portraits gives a feeling of glimpsing the momentum of royal existence, of the sitters in their daily setting. The choice of such locations was made in advance so that electricians and other technicians could set up before he arrived. The routine is caught in his account in 1950 of photographing the infant Princess Anne. In the morning before the sitting he visited Clarence House, then the residence of Princess Elizabeth and the Duke of Edinburgh, where Martin Charteris had shown him the sitting room which it had been suggested would be appropriate. Beaton demurred and proceeded to tour the other possible rooms musing 'columns are always a great asset, and almost every view is flattered when framed by them' (a fact confirmed by his photographs of the Queen Mother in 1957). Although he photographed the Kents at Coppins and at Kensington Palace, the Gloucesters at Barnwell, Princess Alexandra and Angus Ogilvy at Thatched House Lodge, the Royal Family at Windsor Castle and the Queen Mother at Royal Lodge, the only interior which lived up to his demanding criteria for splendid decoration was Buckingham Palace. Although he referred to it as a 'ponderous palace' in 1939 and later in his diaries could be disparaging about the 'frustrating sort of decor you'd see in a grand hotel or attempted on an Atlantic liner' (Diary, March 1960), he continued to respond to it as the essence of regal grandeur and glamour.

In fact, no other photographer either before or since has ever used the State Apartments of Buckingham Palace to such advantage. This major innovation in royal portrait photography has a painterly source, for Beaton must owe something to the celebrated group by Sir John Lavery of King George V and Queen Mary with the Prince of Wales and Princess Royal. This is a Whistlerian nocturne in greys, silvers and golds which translated easily into a photographic tradition of pools and reflections of light first applied by Beaton to the Queen Mother in 1939. For over thirty years he moved through these rooms: the Ballroom, the West Gallery, the Blue Drawing Room, the White and Green Drawing Rooms, the Picture Gallery and the Throne Room. He made abundant use of the grand vistas, of the light which flooded in through the tall windows, of the glint and glitter of gilt and crystal, of the reflections in the mirror glass doors and of the huge formal portraits of bygone kings and queens as well as the wonderful tapestries, bordered curtains and huge tassels. It is striking that he used the garden only once, in 1939, although in 1960 at his suggestion he photographed Princess Margaret on her wedding day on one of the balconies in the inner courtyard, a location he re-used eight years later for his last pictures of the Queen and Prince Charles.

The artificial backgrounds, the royal architecture and the flowers gave Beaton's pictures a remarkable visual coherence through the years. From the mid-1930s to the late 1950s content and style are remarkably uniform. Continuity is also apparent for another reason that had nothing to do with Beaton and to which he practically never refers, the contribution made by the couturier Norman Hartnell. Hartnell dressed most female members of the Royal Family for over three decades. On great state occasions such as the Coronation in 1953 he designed virtually every dress, which accounts for the resulting harmony of the tableaux. Hartnell, like Beaton, worked in theatre and was skilled in orchestrating what was in fact a royal crowd sequence, when colours and cut must compliment each other and in which the Monarch's clothes must be seen to be most resplendent. Hartnell was drawn into royal service at the same time as Beaton. His first contact with the Royal Family was in 1935 when he designed the wedding dress of Lady Alice Montagu-Douglas-Scott on her marriage to the Duke of Gloucester. Subsequently he was taken up by the Duchess of York (later the Queen and Queen Mother) and Queen Mary, who inspired him to study the historic dresses in the Royal School of Needlework.

Hartnell's chance came, however, when he was summoned to the Palace to create the new Queen's wardrobe for the State Visit to Paris in 1938. George VI showed him the royal portraits, especially those by Winterhalter, and out of this came the decision to revive the crinoline. That archaizing decision must have been affected by other influences. One was the celebration of the centenary of Queen Victoria's accession the previous year, when the crinoline was seen on stage in quantity in Rex Whistler's designs for Laurence Housman's play *Victoria Regina* at the Lyric Theatre. No less important was the establishment of the new Queen's style as the antithesis to the modernistic chic of the Duchess of Windsor. It was instead an evocation of *ancien régime* grandeur and high glamour overlaid by 1930s romantic revivalism. Because of the death of the Queen's mother, the entire wardrobe for Paris had at the last minute to be conceived in white, a revival of that colour for mourning, something which only served to heighten the clothes' lustrous, ethereal and other-worldly quality. What in retrospect is so astonishing is that this style of dress was revived in the postwar period. From Princess Elizabeth's wedding dress onwards, Hartnell designed a long sequence of fairytale dresses in the crinoline and New Look styles. Indeed, that visual uniformity of dress, jewels and orders for grand occasions was to be maintained until it finally broke down with the advent of the Princess of Wales and a younger generation in the 1980s. Hartnell died in 1979, only a few months before Beaton.

Lost loveliness

The photographer Edward Steichen criticized Beaton in 1928 for thinking of photography too much in terms of painting. This is amply borne out by the evidence of the Royal portraits. The twin stars in Beaton's firmament were the court painter Franz Xaver Winterhalter and Thomas Gainsborough. The former he refers to as early as 1937 when he photographed Princess Marina 'like a Winterhalter painting', two years before the famous sitting of the Queen in the dresses made by Hartnell directly inspired by the painter. In 1948 Beaton deliberately composed the same sitter into a pastiche of Winterhalter's *Empress Eugénie* and, in the years immediately following, the painter was alluded to again in the lyrical portraits of Princess Margaret. Winterhalter also recurs in many of Beaton's postwar portraits of Princess Marina attired in tiara, evening dress and jewels against a painted cloth of pillars and swags. This rediscovery of Winterhalter sprang naturally out of 1930s romanticism as it pervaded both theatre and cinema. No other artist had created such poetic images of the lost loveliness of vanished courts, of beautiful women in spangled crinolines of lace and tulle adorned with diamond tiaras, stars, necklaces and bracelets. Moreover, following the lead given by George VI, such an allusion emphasized the continuity of the British monarchy after the Abdication. Winterhalter had painted Queen Victoria, Prince Albert and their children as well as Beaton's heroine, Queen Alexandra. In the portraits where this is the over-riding allusion, the resulting images are resonant of a golden past, creating a visual succession of Queens and Princesses, all radiant and ethereal: Victoria, Alexandra, Elizabeth of Glamis, Marina of Greece and the second Elizabeth.

Beaton's obsession with Gainsborough is perhaps even more revealing. It was compulsive: one of his earliest fancy-dress appearances was as Gains-borough and his play about Gainsborough's daughters, *Gainsborough Girls*, was to occupy his mind from 1948 to 1974. His identification with the painter places him in a line of descent in British portraiture stretching back to Van Dyck, one heady with romance and aristocratic dalliance. Occasionally one can pin-point a direct borrowing from the artist, as when he poses the young Princesses Elizabeth and Margaret to resemble a portrait of the painter's two daughters. Generally, however, the similarity is more a matter of mood and general pose. Many of the portraits of the Queen Mother suggest Gainsborough, as Beaton seats her in contemplative mood wearing a silvery dress against a romantic background or makes her gently stroll just turning her head towards the viewer. The pictures of her seated in a crinoline inevitably evoke portraits such as Gainsborough's 'Perdita' Robinson and were surely meant to. The tradition of Reynolds, Lawrence and Sargent has a much harder feel. Gainsborough is all softness and transparency, a fairytale arcadian world lit by a silvery light, one which elides straight into Beaton's soft-focus fantasies. And, as in the case of Winterhalter, the Royal Collection is rich in his works, including portraits of George III, Queen Charlotte and their many children.

At no time was Beaton's sense of the historic past more keenly aroused than at the Coronation in 1953. For the Coronation ceremonies of 1911 and 1937

the photographs had been uninspiring line-ups in the State Apartments of Buckingham Palace, groups totally devoid of any imaginative compositional sense or historical allusion. Drawing on the long tradition of royal portraiture in which the Monarch was depicted in robes of state against a background of grand drapery and columns with a distant view of, for example, one of the royal palaces, he set about constructing a set. The Queen alone was photographed against a blow-up of Henry VII's Chapel in Westminster Abbey, crowned and bearing orb and sceptre. All the other sitters were deployed before a view of the exterior of the Abbey glimpsed through looped curtains. The positioning of these groups and the arrangement of the enormous embroidered velvet and ermine trains betray an attempt to place these pictures in the context of such state portraits as Reynolds's *Queen Charlotte* or Sir George Hayter's *Queen Victoria*.

What, however, prevents his photographs being mere pastiches of historic portraiture is his use of light. In portraits by Winterhalter or Gainsborough the sitter is usually lit from the front, with a mysterious glowing radiance in the background. Beaton, in contrast, frequently orchestrates both natural and artificial light to achieve *contre jour* effects which frame the sitters in an aureole of light. In many cases they are actually made to radiate it. In this he drew on a centuries-old tradition which invests light with a transcendental quality – a halo, for instance, or a celestial beam falling from the heavens. All these allusions are deployed as the Queen Mother is made to float in shafts of real sunlight, or Princess Margaret is posed in front of a battery of concealed lights that suggest a rising sun. These techniques he owed above all to the photography of Baron Gayne de Meyer, whose fashion and portrait photographs he had admired from youth: 'He invented a new universe: a high-key world of water sparkling with sunshine, of moonlight and candlelight, of water lilies in glass bowls, of pearly lustre and dazzling sundrops filtered through lustrous branches. He was able to reproduce the mystery of a Whistlerian nocturne by means of the camera' (*Magic Image*, p. 106). Beaton went on repeating these effects right into the 1960s, for example in his pictures of Princess Alexandra amidst the fluttering leaves of a weeping tree.

Reflective surfaces also fascinated him and these, whether wood or mirror glass, are a motif that from his very earliest royal portraits, of Prince George looking into a glass in 1932, down to Prince Charles in 1968 caught in the reflection of the huge mirror glass doors of the State Apartments of Buckingham Palace. In a 1961 photograph of Princess Alice, Duchess of Gloucester, he is even able to make use of folding looking-glass doors to achieve a triple portrait of the sitter (with himself caught camera in hand within it too).

Painters were not to be the only influences. The photographers Beaton sought to emulate in the middle of the 1920s attracted international society and royalty to their studios. Beaton learnt something from all of them. Marcus Adams's studies of royal and upper-class children in the manner of Gainsborough and Reynolds were influential. The enormously successful Bertram Park lavished aureoles of burnished gold on his sitters of a kind Beaton was to imitate. Indeed, his earliest reference to a royal photograph is to one by Park. In July 1924 the entire Beaton family made a visit to Sandringham, where he caught a glimpse of his heroine Queen Alexandra ('For me, she had always been a fantastic figure from an unbelievable past grandeur'), then a frail but still beautiful old lady. Beaton peered through one of the ground floor windows: 'I caught a glimpse of the old Queen pottering about the sitting room. Stopping at a crowded table she picked up a silver-framed photograph of the Duke and Duchess of York, taken by Bertram Park in soft focus.' Beaton readily assimilated the current practices of the fashionable portrait photographers of the day and went on to be influenced by more distinguished international photographers and, later in life, to respond to the innovations of a younger generation. In the 1930s the main influences were Steichen and Hoyningen-Huene, both of whom were colleagues on *Vogue*. Their influence is felt in what might be categorized as his 'Windsor Style' of photography, the antithesis of the romanticism he was to use from 1939 onwards for the Royal Family. His earliest royal sitters, the Kents and the Duchess of Gloucester, are presented in both modes. Princess Marina in one sitting is depicted in a neo-rococo idyll and in another appears as a smart-set beauty in classic 1930s draperies embracing a Corinthian capital exploding with paper flowers. Similarly the Duchess of Gloucester is presented dreaming against his Fragonard backcloth in tiara and jewels while in other pictures she becomes a pale face emerging from the shadows in the manner of a Steichen portrait. What is important is the parting of the ways, for the use of strong contrasts of light and shade, sharp lines and an unequivocally contemporary vision was, from 1939 onwards, to be reserved for the Windsors alone. From that date until the close of the 1950s the Royal Family were interpreted almost entirely in neo-romantic terms. The only interruption was the war, when Beaton was unable to use splendid dresses and jewels and consequently found it difficult to create interesting royal portraits. Neo-romanticism was promptly resurrected in 1945 and continued for over a decade.

The transformation

The seeming abandonment of this painterly style was brought about by two pressures. One was the need for the monarchy to shift its public image towards greater informality, a movement which began in the late 1950s after public criticism and was to continue throughout the 1960s. Secondly, there was the threat of a new generation of photographers. No sooner had the Duke of Edinburgh's protégé, Baron, died in 1956 than Antony Armstrong-Jones, later Lord Snowdon, appeared. Ironically, bearing in mind the loyalty of that family to Beaton, it was the young Duke of Kent who first commissioned Armstrong-Jones, in 1956. A year later he photographed the entire Royal Family in the grounds of Buckingham Palace. Beaton was unnerved and wrote to his secretary: 'I don't think A. A. Jones's pictures are at all interesting but his publicity value is terrific. It pays to be new in the field.'

Although his rival was for a time 'cancelled out' by his marriage to Princess Margaret in 1960, the fact that he was commissioned at all reflected a desire to find a new photographer who could convey a new image. By that date the painterly manner was hopelessly outmoded and in response to this Beaton developed an informal style which was heavily influenced by Irving Penn and Richard Avedon. All the old props were jettisoned as he placed members of the Royal Family in front of rolls of seamless white paper or took them out into the open air. Princess Margaret and Princess Alexandra with their husbands and children are captured in a sunlit arcadia reminiscent of an Impressionist painting: Gainsborough and Winterhalter might be said to have given way to Renoir and Pissarro. Even the Queen was taken out on to one of the balconies of the internal courtyard of Buckingham Palace in 1968. More than that, the Queen Mother was photographed for her seventieth birthday not in crinoline and tiara but in the gardens of Royal Lodge. Yet the most successful picture was one in which Beaton placed her against a bank of rhododendron blooms, using them in exactly the same way that thirty years before he had used his old Fragonard background.

Beaton was sixty-six in 1970, the year in which he took those photographs. The end of his long reign came three years later when Norman Parkinson photographed Princess Anne and Captain Mark Phillips on the eve of their marriage. Parkinson went on to take the wedding photographs and, after Beaton's stroke in 1974, to assume his mantle, covering the Queen Mother's seventy-fifth and eightieth birthdays and the Queen's Silver Jubilee as well as photographing most other members of the Royal Family. Beaton, however, never gave up. Shortly before he died he wrote to the Queen Mother asking whether he might take her eightieth birthday pictures. But death intervened.

In one sense, by the early 1970s if not before, Beaton was the relic of an earlier era. He never fully responded to the new direction taken by the Crown. None the less, his work for the House of Windsor over four decades still stands as a unique monument to a relationship between a royal family and an artist of a kind familiar from earlier centuries. And that is precisely how he saw himself, as a latter-day Gainsborough waving his wand of mystery and beauty. No other royal photographer has been charged with such a sense of history or been so supremely successful at ennobling his sitters. Beaton's work sprang from a profound loyalty to the concept of the monarchy. However much his indiscreet and occasionally wicked pen would prick holes in the Royal Family in his diaries, that never affected his work. He always had a keen sense that every royal person is two — an embodiment of an abstract principle in a fallible human shell. Beaton was a passionate monarchist. I remember going to lunch with him at Reddish in 1977 shortly after the Silver Jubilee and describing it to him. Tears of emotion ran down his face as I depicted the scene outside Buckingham Palace at night when the Queen appeared on the palace balcony.

Like the great court painters of the past Beaton conceived his role to be the transmutation of his sitters into personifications of his country. He saw the men as handsome and the women as beautiful and through the manipulation of light and of his camera's lens he made them so. Beaton as a result was one of the key image-makers of the British monarchy as it came to terms with the pressures of democracy and the collapse of the *ancien régime* in the rest of Europe and Russia after World War I. Through the distribution of his pictures by means of the mass circulation of newspapers and magazines, the idea of monarchy in late twentieth-century Britain was fashioned and formulated. As Harold Nicolson wrote, 'Too much publicity will stain the mystery, even the dignity of the Crown. Too little publicity will be regarded as undemocratic and will render the gulf between the sovereign and the ordinary subject an unfortunate barrier rather than a necessity of segregation.' Beaton completely overcame this problem. His pictures embody the history and tradition of centuries, evoking in the eye of the viewer a sense of continuity, tradition and glory. To these he added the new ingredient of humanity which a more democratic age demanded. His sitters remained kings and queens, princes and princesses, dukes and duchesses, but they are also, through his lens, mothers and fathers, sons and daughters, widows and babies. He gave to royalty the element of common humanity, but mystery was maintained; for the first time grandeur came with a smile. That delicate balance Beaton never betrayed in what will always remain the greatest alliance ever forged between crown and camera.

The final stage

The end of the process of taking a royal portrait was its
publication in newspapers and magazines throughout the
world. It is a tribute to Beaton's photographs that they look as
much at home on the front cover of a mass-market magazine
as in a silver frame in a drawing room.

THE ILLUSTRATED LONDON NEWS

The World Copyright of all the Editorial Matter, both Illustrations and Letterpress, is Strictly Reserved in Great Britain, the British Dominions and Colonies, Europe, and the United States of America.

SATURDAY, JUNE 23, 1956.

SOVEREIGN OF THE MOST NOBLE ORDER OF THE GARTER : HER MAJESTY THE QUEEN.

On June 18 her Majesty the Queen, Sovereign of the Most Noble Order of the Garter, attended the annual service of the Order at St. George's Chapel, Windsor, at which three Knight Companions—Sir Anthony Eden, Earl Attlee and the Earl of Iveagh were installed. This striking

Postage—Inland, 3d.; Canada, 1½d.; Elsewhere Abroad, 3½d. (These rates apply at The Illustrated London News is registered at the G.P.O. as a newspaper.)

photograph of the Queen shows her Majesty wearing the Habit and Ensigns of the Order, which was founded by King Edward III in about 1348. The last installation ceremony held at Windsor was that of Sir Winston Churchill in June 1954. [Photograph by Cecil Beaton.]

Look

Jack Dempsey Picks
The Man Who Could Beat Louis

The Story Behind 'The Grapes of Wrath'

How to Crash the Windsors' Set

AUGUST 29, 1939 10¢

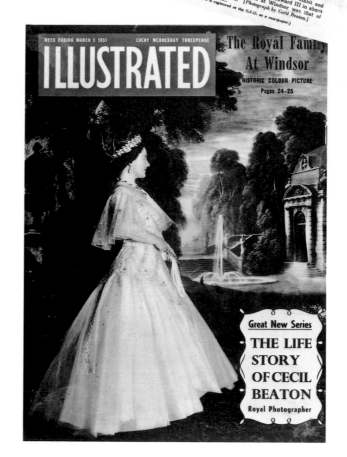

Queen Elizabeth · Special Article Inside

Woman's Own

3D
Every
Friday
Aug. 10. 1940

Photograph
by
Cecil Beaton

WEEK ENDING MARCH 3 1951   EVERY WEDNESDAY THREEPENCE

ILLUSTRATED

The Royal Family
At Windsor
HISTORIC COLOUR PICTURE
Pages 24-25

Great New Series
**THE LIFE
STORY
OF CECIL
BEATON**
Royal Photographer

Before Beaton

A glimpse of royal portrait photographs before Beaton's arrival helps to make clear his achievement. This stiffly posed Coronation photograph of George V and Queen Mary in 1911 (right) seems ungainly in comparison with his 1953 Coronation portraits. Part of his secret was the ability to combine the directness of everyday portraiture with the formality of a state portrait, such as that of his heroine Queen Alexandra (above, a photograph from Beaton's own collection). Even so, he added a glamour all of his own. Eight years after the Duchess of York posed for the photograph top right she unexpectedly became Queen, but it took Beaton's vision to transform her from the sweet motherly lady of 1928 into the romantic beauty overleaf.

THE ROYAL
PORTRAITS

ONE
THE IDYLL
1930—1939

ONLY A YEAR AFTER THE TRIUMPHANT CELEBRATIONS for George V's Silver Jubilee in 1935, the monarchy was profoundly shaken by the King's death and the Abdication crisis. When Edward VIII decided to abandon the throne for the sake of Mrs Wallis Warfield Simpson, his place was taken by the Duke and Duchess of York. Their accession as George VI and Queen Elizabeth was greeted with some anxiety. They had been given a role that was not of their choosing: would they rise to the awesome challenge? Their success is embodied in Beaton's idyllic photographs. Once his camera had responded to the hard-edged chic of the Duke and Duchess of Windsor and their fashionable friends. Now he showed to the world a very different story: the new Queen, smilingly friendly as well as romantically regal, at Buckingham Palace in the last summer before the war. These happy photographs were to prove an enduringly popular demonstration of the revival of the Royal House of Windsor.

Queen Elizabeth, standing below the Waterloo Vase in the gardens of Buckingham Palace, July 1939.

'EACH EVENING THERE WERE SHOUTING THOUSANDS IN FRONT of the floodlit palace, waiting for Their Majesties to appear smiling and laughing on the balconies. The King and Queen wept and said that they had not before known that they were popular.' Beaton's memory of the 1935 Silver Jubilee celebrations for George V and Queen Mary, recorded in his *Scrapbook* (1937), evokes one of the great triumphs of the British monarchy in the twentieth century. The popularity of the old King and Queen was based in part on two recent developments. The first was their stature as the embodiment of the bourgeois virtues: they were hard-working, Christian and devoted to the simple pleasures of family life. Yet they combined this with a contrasting innovation, the resurgence of royal pageantry that had begun with Queen Victoria's jubilees of 1887 and 1897.

The early years of the century saw the creation or revival of the now-traditional ceremonies of the Order of the Garter, the State Opening of Parliament and the distribution of Royal Maundy money. The Investiture of the Prince of Wales and the lying-in-state of a deceased monarch and his consort were innovations; major events such as coronations, jubilees or visits by foreign heads of state were for the first time marked by vast cavalcades through the streets of London. In 1919 royal weddings, for over a century celebrated in private, returned to the public domain with the marriage of Princess Patricia of Connaught to Captain Alexander Ramsay, followed in 1922 by that of the Princess Royal to Viscount Lascelles and in 1923 by the marriage of the Duke and Duchess of York, all in Westminster Abbey.

None of this would have had such impact if the pageantry had not been deliberately conceived to exploit the new mass circulation of newspapers and magazines with their improved techniques of printing and photography. For the first time photographs of the Royal Family acquired public importance, as the means whereby the world could participate in their ceremonial and private lives. Beaton's royal career was based largely on the need for a photographer who could combine in a single image that mixture of mystery and virtue upon which the power of the monarchy was henceforth to depend.

The Windsor wedding

The accession of Edward VIII on 20 January 1936 was greeted with a tremendous upsurge of good will and expectancy born of his successful apprenticeship as Prince of Wales. His love for the twice-divorced American Mrs Wallis Warfield Simpson and the consequent abdication less than a year after he had become King are now part of twentieth-century mythology. Of particular interest here is the effect that he might have had on the image of the monarchy. His way of life, recently dubbed 'the Windsor Style', was the embodiment of all that his parents disapproved of: the hard chic and rich glamour of the international jet set. The world of the Duke and Duchess of Windsor was one of calculated high fashion, where even informality became an art. Couture clothes by Dior and Givenchy, jewels by Van Cleef & Arpels, an obsession with over-exact interior decoration and a cultivation of café society are some of the hallmarks of their style. It had few elements compatible with the stolid character of the British monarchy as it had evolved since 1900.

This way of life is reflected in Beaton's crisp, elegant photographs of the Duke and Duchess, whom he treated as though they were society figures in the *Tatler* – or even fashion models in *Vogue* – rather than part of the tradition of monarchy. Beaton photographed Wallis Simpson on several occasions before her marriage. He enjoyed her wit and charm and was gratified by the sensation of being at the centre of events. On 2 June 1937, the day before Wallis and the Duke of Windsor were married, Beaton arrived at the Château de Candé in France to take the wedding photographs:

Maurice and the electricians had fixed up the lights in Wallis' bedroom before and we started off by taking the Duke alone. He was very pliable and easy to pose and trying his hardest to make it less difficult for me – He will not allow himself to be photographed on the right side of his face and only likes his parting to be shown. He looked very wrinkled but essentially young and schoolboyish and he had great vitality and keenness. He approved of sitting on a cushion because it was different from the usual chair. He didn't like to be [seen] smoking a cigarette – and his expression though intent was essentially sad, tragic eyes belied by impertinent tilt of nose. He has common hands – like a little mechanic – weather beaten and rather scaly and one thumb-nail is disfigured. His hair at 45 is as golden and thick as it was at 16. His eyes fiercely blue do not seem to focus properly – are bleary in spite of their brightness and one is much lower than another.

When Wallis appeared to be photographed, the Duke was busy looking for a crucifix to put on the improvised altar that had been set up for the next day's ceremony:

The cockney maid telephoned to his room 'Is that Your Royal Highness – well will you please come down right away' and when he did appear Wallis let him see she was annoyed and after a preliminary argument he apologised and the two sat hip to hip on a huge cushion, his far hand round her waist while I photographed the two of them together. The background was a difficulty and over a screen, partly as a joke that I could not resist, I threw the bedspread – a beautiful needlework counterpane of pink satin.

After lunch, the Duke and Wallis changed into their wedding clothes:

Upstairs in the bathroom dressing room hung Wallis' blue wedding dress — and on a stand by the window the hat — a bonnet of pale blue feathers to match with a tulle halo effect. Not a bit pretty but the dress was lovely — and cut very simply and becomingly for the figure. The bath towel was crumpled damply in a corner and on the side of the bath a gillette razor — 'May I look at your jewel case?' and she showed me as much as she could before the next interruption. Her rings are wonderful slabs of diamond, turquoise and emerald. There are layers of velvet covered drawers with so many modern pieces — mostly very beautiful and all very modern settings. The costume ready we took the pictures. 'Oh so this is the great dress — well it's lovely — very pretty' admired the Duke — and I picked a lot of very small pinks from a vase to make it look as if he had a big carnation buttonhole, but the cockney maid, recovered from her tantrum, produced a carnation of her own — an imitation one which suited perfectly ... The sun poured down — more and more pictures were taken and I hated Wallis' hat but didn't say so — and was so glad to be gettting so much good material — at the beginning of the day had thought it impossible to do much.

The Fairy Queen

On Edward VIII's abdication, the Crown passed to George V's second son, Prince Albert, Duke of York, who succeeded as George VI. The monarchy had been badly shaken by the Abdication and keen thought must have been given to its future image. The choice of the name George for the new king signalled a reaffirmation of the popular balance achieved by his father between domestic virtue and public grandeur, but at their accession the Duke and Duchess of York had no very definite public face. The King, less handsome and outgoing than his brothers Windsor and Kent, suffered from a stammer. Partly as a result, the Queen was to be the major focus for the rehabilitation of the royal image. She had been born Lady Elizabeth Bowes-Lyon, the fourth daughter of the 14th Earl of Strathmore and Kinghorne. She married the Duke of York in Westminster Abbey on 26 April 1923 and gradually established herself thereafter as a woman of strong character with a charm that endeared her to the public and to her parents-in-law. Her position was further enhanced by the birth of two daughters, Princess Elizabeth in 1926 and Princess Margaret in 1930.

Beaton owed his invitation to photograph the new Queen to the Duchess of Kent's sister-in-law, Princess Paul of Yugoslavia, who sat for Beaton at Buckingham Palace in July 1939. She was so pleased with the results that she encouraged the Queen to sit as well. Later that month, much to Beaton's amazement, he was summoned to the Palace to discuss the settings and costumes for a sitting that was to produce an enduring new fairytale image for the Queen:

We went to the wing occupied by the King and Queen overlooking Green Park, and through the windows could be heard the changing of the guard and the commands of the officers shouting to their men sounding like someone retching and though the Palace is enormous one has no feeling of remoteness from the people. The garden though enormous is filled with the distant roar of traffic — and through the windows of many rooms one can see the crowds waiting outside the Palace . . .

The Queen is ready now . . . She was very smiling and easy — nevertheless I felt myself standing very stiff and my knees shaking rather. 'It is a great happiness for me Ma'am'. 'It is very exciting for me'. We discussed dresses . . . 'I thought perhaps another evening dress of — tulle? — and a — tiara?' All this very wistfully said and rather apologetically with a smile. I suggested also a garden party dress — with a long skirt — and a different makeup. I would get the different coloured lipstick. 'I'll try but I'm not very good at it you know' — as if to say it was not her line of country. Her arms and wrists were white and rounded — with diamond bracelets and perfumed with tuberose. She is very short and her heels are very high. I liked her — but I feared for the camera results. In the glaring light from the garden windows she looked flat and shadowless — but I went away in high spirits and full of expectations for the afternoon . . .

Beaton returned to the Palace in the afternoon to take the photographs:

At last a rush of pages and a hustle in the corridors and the Queen appeared looking enchanting in a ruby encrusted crinoline of gold and silver. In the yellow drawing room it looked ideal. The superintendant had told me that I wouldn't get long with the Queen — at any rate nothing like it was with Princess Paul — that not since the last King George's reign had any photographer been allowed to take pictures for more than 20 minutes and so from the moment the Queen appeared I photographed with monkeylike frenzy. This seemed to amuse her — and delight her — and stimulate her for from the moment we started she smiled and showed that she was enjoying every moment of it . . .

The background on the screen was changed, I refilled the Rolleiflex which ran out of films so quickly that it became a joke. 'It is empty again?' — and the Queen reappeared in tulle spangled like a fairy doll — and rather apologetically with a smile she admitted I did change the tiara — and these diamonds — are they alright? They were given as a Coronation present by the King and they are diamonds in 2 rows as big as walnuts. When discussing jewelry I had suggested as much should be worn as possible. 'The choice isn't very great you know'. Later the Queen was enjoined to change the diamonds for 3 rows of enormous pearls 'Are three rows too much?' 'Oh no Oh no — ' but a little later she was in a corner unclasping one row and saying with a giggle 'I think 3 is too much!' The plates were used up with appalling rapidity. The Rolleiflex doing splendid duty whenever the big camera was not ready — pictures were taken of the Queen against my Piranesi and Fragonard background with flowers from her rooms padding the sides of her chair, against the pillars of the drawing rooms — in the doorways, on sofas — and then the sun shone for the first time this day and that gave me new inspiration and we took many more lovely pictures that should be very romantic — of the fairy Queen in her ponderous Palace — and the sun gave rise to hopes for photography in the garden — a garden party dress perhaps in the garden? The Queen was game for almost anything and I was so grateful and so pleased — laughing with high spirits and admiration.

After the Queen had changed, the photography continued outside:

Although I had no idea of the time it was in fact six o'clock in the evening — the lawns of the Palace were fitfully strewn with sunlight but the atmosphere and effect was strange and timeless and I felt that this expedition to photograph by the water's edge was something out of reality — something like a dream. The Queen talked hard — I am interested in your photography — You have set such a high standard — Can you do a lot afterwards — Can you take out a whole table — 'A table is a bit much Ma'am but I can slice people in half'. And how the King will laugh when I tell him you photograph me always directly against the sun — we always have to spend our time running round to face the sun for the King's snapshots.

Photography continued under a giant vase in a summer house of tridents that came, so it seems, from the Admiralty. Photography from under the trees against the water and with the Palace in the distance. 'Do you like the house from here?' That central part's the original Buckingham House. Will my parasol outline the Palace? — it's a very long Palace. It's very beautiful and in the opalescent light it looked so very unreal and made of opals. This was [an] opal dream and the Queen must have felt so too otherwise physical exhaustion would have made her go in long before this and it was I who spared her by finally suggesting we had taken enough.

The traffic roar continued and the evening sky was beginning to lose its power and soon the sky would become rose coloured as if, as the Queen said, Piccadilly was afire every night. We walked back to the Palace — tired and baffled officials clustering by the doors. I told the Queen I can't bear to say goodbye — and the Queen said it would be very exciting when the package arrived — and so a charming experience was ended and downstairs in the circular hall I took my leave. As mementoes of the experience, there would be a hundred photographs but in my pocket was hidden and scented with tuberoses and gardenias, a handkerchief that the Queen had tucked behind the cushion of the chair away from the onslaught of the camera lenses — A relic of the occasion that will have much more Romance and reality than any of the photographs.

The fashionable Kents

Prince George, Duke of Kent, was the fourth son of George V and Queen Mary. A man of considerable good looks and great personal magnetism, he shared with his mother a passion for collecting and the arts. Much of his early life remains obscure (there is no biography of him), for it involved not only unsuitable girl friends and drug addiction but even (it was rumoured) homosexual relationships and blackmail. In 1934 he married Princess Marina, one of the three daughters of Prince Nicholas of Greece and Helen, daughter of Grand Duke Vladimir of Russia. When Greece was declared a republic in 1923 her family had moved to France, from where they made frequent visits to London. There Marina attracted the attention of her godmother, Queen Mary, on the look-out for a possible bride for the Prince of Wales. However, Marina fell in love with the Prince's youngest brother and their wedding, after a whirlwind romance, attracted huge public attention.

As a couple they were made for Beaton to photograph and he responded enthusiastically to their beauty and sense of style. In his diary he wrote an account of their sitting for him in the spring of 1937 at their house in Belgrave Square:

The Duchess looked excessively beautiful in a huge brown tulle crinoline, ruched like a Queen Anne window blind — or a lampshade — with old fashioned diamond jewelry — a bow knot — large drop earrings . . . The arrival of the Duke created a nervous tension as he seemed to be in a bad mood and there is no one bloodier than he in a bad mood — cantankerous, cross like a spoilt schoolboy and today he looked as though he had stepped out of bed the wrong side having lain in it only too little — and not subsequently having bothered to shave. He was late already — would she change and then they'd be done together and in the mean time he could have some done alone.

In the last few years his beauty has deteriorated sadly. He no longer resembles Queen Alexandra with huge aquamarine eyes and pink lips. His eyes are now tired and strained like his father's. His complexion less pink and white and like a forgotten apple with crinkles on it. However, he has beauty — great style and is extremely attractive. Our most attractive male Royalty by far — and he has wit and a sense of humour but today he didn't ease matters and I was delighted after a bad start, to get the atmosphere warmed up, to make him amused . . .

When the choice of which photograph should be sent to each magazine the Duchess said 'and do you want to be in Vogue or Sketch and Tatler'. 'Oh I hate to be in the Sketch and Tatler — Vogue.' 'But Vogue is a fashion magazine' — to which the Duke snarled his very attractive snorting laugh (screwed nose) 'Well what about it? Aren't we fashionable?'

A difficult Duchess

Lady Alice Montagu-Douglas-Scott, the third daughter of the 7th Duke of Buccleuch, married Prince Henry, Duke of Gloucester, in 1935. He was the third son of George V and Queen Mary. Beaton photographed the Duchess in 1935 and 1938. There is no diary entry for the first sitting and an exceptionally abrasive one for the second. As Beaton's biographer remarks, 'Although she was the sort of person Cecil might well have liked, the Duchess of Gloucester was never his favourite royal sitter, perhaps because she criticized his work' (Vickers, p. 196). The day began badly with Beaton, suffering from an appalling cold, being booked for speeding on his way to the sitting at York House, part of St James's Palace:

I had had a very pretty background copied from the Fragonard 'Swing' in the Wallace [Collection] so was full of expectation for the best. My hopes were dashed the moment when Her Royal Highness walked into the room. She had had her hair waved with such hot irons that it was frizzy and the waves at the crown were as tight as tinned anchovies . . . The diamond and turquoise parure added no glamour . . . Her face colourless without expression was a hopeless job . . . I tried after the first cold douche of the Duchess's appearance (never a howdydo as she entered) to take the lead and keep up a running commentary but by degrees I gave up all attempts at lightening the burden of the afternoon and photographed her as an inanimate object . . .

Each time I snatched at her cloak, at a flower from a basket she would look horrified and her idiotic lady in waiting would come to her aid. I don't think that'll do that any good. I explained that I always wreaked damage when I was photographing and I then became less polite and asked if there were no better flowers in the house (a very scratch selection) and they apologised. Do I look in the Kodak? Do I put my eyes in the Kodak? Yes — yes — well I'd like one with the dogs for my friends and a formal one in tiara and orders for the Dominions and my husband likes to have a special one for himself that no one else has. His own special one for his desk. Yes — it's best to take as many as possible at once so we can choose from a lot . . .

Really the atmosphere was so drab and depressing — I loathed the house, the rooms, the camera, the background . . . I left a wreck — For a week I was in bed with a terrible cold and the physical strain must have been one of the reasons for my collapse. The proofs came and were even worse than I had imagined. Heaven only knows what anyone else will think.

In fact the results were a great success.

The Duke of Windsor and Mrs Simpson at the Château de Candé, near Tours, where they were married on 3 June 1937.

The Windsor wedding

Cecil Beaton, Wallis Simpson, the Duke of Windsor and his devoted equerry Major Edward Dudley Metcalfe, standing against the Gothic balustrade seen in the previous picture. Wallis's blue silk wedding outfit was designed by Mainbocher; her hat — which Beaton disliked so much — was by Caroline Reboux. A pink bedspread was used as an improvised backdrop for some of the photographs (right).

Overleaf: *Wallis in another couture outfit, this time by Schiaparelli; the Duke's attention to elegant dressing is no less marked.*

'The pictures taken on the steps and terrace of the stone porch should be the most successful for the
Equerry brought some bad news during the time the pictures at the turret window were being taken.'
This was probably the information that Wallis would not be granted royal status on her marriage.

Looking back on this sitting, Beaton reflected that Wallis was 'determined to love the Duke, though I feel she is not in love with him. She has a great responsibility in looking after someone who, so essentially different, relies entirely upon her.'

The Fairy Queen

Beaton's celebrated photographs of Queen Elizabeth at Buckingham Palace in 1939 established a new romantic image for the monarchy. Turning away from the smartly modern Duke and Duchess of Windsor, the Queen appears as an idyllic figure from a Victorian fairytale, dressed in a shimmering crinoline decked with diamonds.

'In the daylight now she looked a dream — but what when the electric lamps were ablaze? They went on in a flash and to my utter amazement and joy the Queen looked a dream — a porcelain doll — with flawless little face like luminous china in front of a fire. Her smile as fresh as a dewdrop — her regard uncompromising and kindly — altogether a face that reveals what the owner is — someone with the best instincts — strict in her likes — gay — sympathetic — witty — shrewd — wistful and so well educated that she makes one full of admiration rather than shame. She is a great lady — and childish — an angel with genius and she makes every man feel she needs his protection though she can well get along on her own merits.'

In this photograph the Queen wears a silk tulle crinoline scattered with sequin spangles, designed by Norman Hartnell.

Overleaf: Two studies of the Queen dressed in another Hartnell dress, of heavy cream satin with a gold lamé underskirt, the yoke of the bodice and the sweeping side panels thickly covered with metallic embroidery. With it she wears the 'Indian' tiara and necklace made for Queen Victoria in 1853, a diamond tassel brooch which came from Queen Alexandra's collection, the Garter star and sash and the Garter itself on her arm.

N.S. No. 4.

N.S. No. 5.

N.S. No. 6.

N.S. No. 7.

N.S. No. 8.

N.S. No. 9.

A selection of the officially approved photographs from the sitting, released to the press in two series, in December 1939 and March 1940. The Queen is dressed in the Hartnell crinoline in which she appears on page 61, but here it is worn with a diamond fringe tiara made in 1830 from jewels that had belonged to George III. The two diamond necklaces were both made for Queen Victoria; one is of 28 and the other of 45 collet stones. The pendant stone and the earring drops came from the Treasury of Lahore and were presented by the East India Company to Queen Victoria in 1851.

Overleaf: *The Queen in the Blue Drawing Room at Buckingham Palace. 'The Queen could see the reflection in the mirrors and was very pleased herself with the effect and like a pretty child pleased with a new party dress beamed with contentment.'*

In the late afternoon of the sitting, the Queen descends the steps of Buckingham Palace and wanders about the grounds for Beaton's camera. Wearing a garden-party dress designed by Hartnell for a state visit to Paris in 1938, she first pauses beside the Waterloo Vase, carved by Sir Richard Westmacott to commemorate the victory over Napoleon, and then poses between the caryatids of an eighteenth-century summer house.

These idyllic photographs were felt to be out of keeping with the mood of a country which declared war only two months after they were taken. None was published until the 1960s.

'The sky was now cloudy though opalescent sun did come through at intervals — and the sun came out for the Queen as she appeared smiling and laughing in a tempest on the terrace. She was wearing a champagne coloured garden party dress and hat and parasol — and loving it — a delighted porcelain doll — and a delighted shrewd and witty woman. She walked in the tempest while I ran about with a small camera and in the distance were the attendant men so that the Queen really felt at liberty to talk easily and was here at her best ... Do you like this parasol as much as I do — It belonged to Catherine of Russia — and it's so like her — so gold and encrusted with jewels — and it was her stick — Do you think she would mind my using it as a Parasol — which is a symbol of all summer — and leisure.'

The fashionable Kents

The Duke of Kent was one of Beaton's earliest royal patrons. In 1932 he sat for a series of elegantly
self-absorbed portraits reminiscent of Beaton's photographs of film-stars. Such very unconventional
pictures of a royal prince were not for public release. Princess Marina of Greece, the Duchess of Kent,
photographed above in 1938, remained one of Beaton's favourite sitters for over thirty years. 'Those who
had the good fortune to meet her,' he wrote after her death in 1968, 'could see the cool classical features
in a perfect oval head held high on a straight column of neck, the topaz eyes, the slightly tilted smile, the
apricot complexion, and the nut-brown cap of flat silken curls.'

The Duke and Duchess, photographed at their home in Belgrave Square in 1937.

'While the two were photographed he struck me as leading her a terrible dance. Once she said my hair won't go in the right shape — it's most annoying. To which "It's not annoying to me I don't care a bit". Sometimes he'd put his tongue out at her but if she unseen gave him a poke he would bring it out into daylight and explain "Don't poke me like that — it's not funny and not helpful to the photographs". Later we took many pictures of the Duchess — in Greek draperies holding aloft an empty easel on which her beloved will be superimposed.'

Two more photographs from the same sitting, showing how at this date Beaton's contemporary and neo-romantic modes could be used interchangeably on the same royal sitter. He remembered that she was 'slightly nervous at first and very Royal, with her deep clipped accented voice — but soon she was as pliable as any sitter I have ever had and we made many jokes and got along splendidly'.

With her Greek costume the Duchess wears a five-row choker made from 373 oriental pearls which had belonged to Queen Mary. It was a wedding gift from her husband.

The Duchess sat for Beaton again in 1938 and he later recalled how she arrived at his studio bearing 'a picnic lunch-basket and boxes containing Greek national dress and her formal gown complete with orders and decorations'. The resulting photographs are among Beaton's most romantic royal portraits.

The photograph above was taken at Buckingham Palace in 1939. The Duchess wears part of the magnificent sapphire and diamond parure given to her by Queen Mary. On the right is another photograph from her 1937 sitting. The diamond bow was a present from Tsar Nicholas II to her mother, Helen, daughter of Grand Duke Vladimir of Russia, on her marriage to Prince Nicholas of Greece in 1902.

A difficult Duchess

The Duchess of Gloucester proved an awkward sitter when Beaton photographed her in 1938, but the results were excellent. The portraits fall into two groups: the first with evening dress and turquoise parure in a neo-romantic vein, the second (overleaf) in a more contemporary mode.

'I asked that she put on more makeup, that the lips should be darkened and enlarged but suddenly an overwhelming inertia took hold of me — I could not struggle. It was the nightmare where one is chased and one's feet are caught in treacle ... In a fierce effort to get some good results I banked on quantity ... dozens of photographs were taken.'

TWO

THE WAR

1939—1945

No sooner had Beaton so successfully established a new image for the monarchy than the outbreak of war on 3 September 1939 meant a complete and sudden change. Throughout the six years of conflict, the King and Queen and their daughters set an example of unstinting duty, sharing the restrictions of food rationing and clothing coupons with their subjects. Court life and pageantry went into abeyance and there were no occasions for Beaton's formal portrayal of bejewelled royalty. Instead his photographs emphasize as never before the Royal Family's ordinariness, an image of unity in a time of national adversity. Only as the struggle drew to its close did the beautiful young Princesses Elizabeth and Margaret emerge as symbols of a brighter future, allowing Beaton at last to return to the romantic style he had created.

Princess Elizabeth at the age of sixteen, wearing the insignia of the Grenadier Guards, whose Colonel-in-Chief she became in 1942.

BY THE TIME THAT BEATON'S IDYLLIC PHOTOGRAPHS OF THE Queen were published, in December 1939, war had been declared. He was worried that they were inappropriate to wartime, but perhaps because of their remoteness from everyday concerns they were immensely popular. One of the portraits of the Queen in her tiara appeared on the Christmas card sent in the King and Queen's name to every man and woman serving in the armed forces: an image of what the country was fighting for.

In retrospect it is taken for granted that the Royal Family should have stayed in the country for the duration of the war, but quite early on the Cabinet formally advised the King that Princesses Elizabeth and Margaret should be evacuated to Canada, just as many other families were sending their children out of harm's way. The Queen famously replied that her daughters would never leave the country without her and that she would never leave without the King, 'and the King will never leave'.

The Royal Family suffered many of the same deprivations as their subjects. Mrs Roosevelt, visiting Buckingham Palace in 1942, commented on the freezing temperatures in the bedrooms and the austerity food – which even so was served on silver plates. During the Battle of Britain, on 15 September 1940, a German Bomber daringly flew straight down the Mall, and dropped six bombs on Buckingham Palace and its grounds, causing considerable damage but no loss of life. One of the Queen's nephews was killed in action and another was taken prison of war.

The arrival of Churchill as Prime Minister in May 1940 was not warmly greeted by the King and Queen, perhaps in part because they remembered his enthusiastic support for Edward VIII during the Abdication crisis. Although by the end of the war they had formed a warm alliance, George VI was replaced to a great extent in the public imagination by Winston Churchill as the personification of the nation at war. There was a slippage from the wave of adulation for the monarchy that had followed the accession in 1936 and although there was always a loyal following for the King's hesitant but deeply sincere Christmas broadcasts, it was Churchill's radio speeches which stirred the nation. Strangely, the Royal Family was regarded with a certain amount of indifference, if not disaffection, as their relevance and way of life in wartime began to be questioned and criticized.

None the less, they set an often inspiring example of energetic duty. Their role as leaders of society had of course vanished, as had court life and pageantry. Instead the King and Queen toured areas of destruction caused by enemy bombing (with the result that their presence became unfairly linked with such disasters), inspected munitions factories and reviewed the armed forces. Princess

Elizabeth broadcast to the Empire's children and in 1945 became a subaltern in the Auxiliary Territorial Service. In all the official royal photographs throughout this period the deliberate emphasis as never before was on the family's ordinariness, and they were shown engaged in the simple joys of home life or the domestic trials of war such as practising fire drill. Reluctantly Beaton had to comply with this new down-to-earth image. Only as the struggle drew to its close were the two princesses of an age when he could project them as the embodiment of the better times that it was hoped would come in peace.

1942 : The Royal Family and Mrs Roosevelt

The alliance of the USA and the United Kingdom in the aftermath of Pearl Harbor was symbolized in October 1942 by the visit of Mrs Eleanor Roosevelt. The President's wife came at the invitation of the Queen to inspect the conditions of US troops stationed in England and to see the role played by women in the war effort. Beaton was summoned to photograph her with the Royal Family at Buckingham Palace:

The Royal Family came in quietly and shyly. The King embarrassed and the muscle moving in his cheek. The Queen smiling blandly, the children very meek with furtive sidelong glances. Mrs Roosevelt is just taking her hat off and then she will have a cup of tea and then we'll come in right away. We were ready to take pictures in the Bow Room — with rather pretty medallions containing copies of Winterhalter portraits. The cupboards bare of silver [in fact, porcelain] — and the fireplace empty. The King said 'It's a shame that cupboard being empty isn't it?' Instead of replying 'Yes, but that's a good war time touch Sir.' I said 'if the camera is moved this way the pillar here hides it' — of course when the photograph comes out the King would see that the bare cupboard did show. 'I told Beaton that would show' — and I had successfully put myself in the wrong. Mrs Roosevelt appeared enormous over life size in fact with a roving smile and eyes that never focused anywhere. She was elephant coloured — no particular stress or emphasis in any feature — her hair nondescript . . . it was only much later after reading of it in the Press that any of us realised how deaf Mrs Roosevelt has become. This deafness is an appalling disadvantage for it means that she has the look and the voice of a deaf person.

Obviously it made no difference to her how she looked in pictures. Personal vanity is something of which she is not conscious. She hurried as soon as possible to go upstairs and write 'Her Day'. Then the Royal Family were photographed. The King quite amenable . . . a good man — wouldn't do a bad thing. Peppery — but . . . without any mystery or magic whatsoever. One forgets after a few minutes that he is in the room. The Queen was as divinely sympathetic and full of charm as ever and quite witty — slightly mischevious about

Mrs R. and the Americans. She imagined Mrs R. would not keep still thinking she must keep animated for the movie camera! I suggested she had no repose — 'Oh but she has much animation'. The King was photographed in one corner of the room where the enormous Chinese vase covered with dragons was surmounting a niche. This is a strange object to have lit upon. I suggested that it casts nice shadows — Isn't it hideous — where did it come from I wonder. After we had surveyed it for some seconds in silence the King ventured 'It's Chinese I suppose.'

The photography lasted longer that I had supposed and the voluntary woman driver waiting to take the films to be developed (super rush order) sent in a note to say she had waited 20 minutes — couldn't stay any longer tonight. I was enthusiastic to see how very much more charming Princess Elizabeth has become than any of the photographs I have seen of her. She has her mother's smile — is extremely well brought up — and has a great knowledge of history. They made quite charming pictures — and together the Princesses reminded me of the beginning of my photographic career when I used to photograph Nancy and Baba [his sisters] as school children.

Beaton returned to the Palace on 30 October:

It was arranged to photograph the Queen and the Princesses again in one week's time. I arrived at the Palace this time full of confidence. I knew the Queen would as ever be helpful — and kind. I looked forward to the sitting with great glee. The electrician had told me on arrival that he must leave with his lights at 4.30 — for a Vogue Pattern Book sitting. This was such that it entirely upset my peace of mind — and also I never regained it — of course I could not allow him to leave — but I did not have his cooperation or enthusiasm. He was bored with the Queen — the Princesses. The whole thing. He was never on the spot with the lights at the right time. For 3 hours I sweated like a bull. It was one of the hardest afternoons I have ever spent — it was not a success — inspite of wonderful cooperation from Queen and children — all the time I felt like a singer with a bad accompaniment — or in the nightmare when one's feet are treading in treacle as one is being chased by a murderer. The Queen was extremely sympathetic and helpful — but ... I was too rattled with the photographic side to hear any interesting anecdotes or remarks — except that I was amused to hear the Queen say of her dress — It's what I call a nothing colour.

Windsor in wartime

Beaton photographed the Royal Family at Windsor Castle in November 1943 and the pictures were released to mark Princess Elizabeth's eighteenth birthday on 21 April 1944. The photographer himself suggested Windsor as a setting because Buckingham Palace had been used so often.

Sir Eric Mieville [the Queen's Private Secretary] rang up midday Saturday to say the Queen was expecting me to take pictures of the family at Windsor on the Monday morning. To be there at 11 o'clock to photograph the princesses in the morning — the King and Queen in the afternoon. This meant an appalling rush of last minute arrangements in the face of difficulties. Even in war time most people are away on Saturday — However, we started off in time on a pouring wet day — dark and foggy. I drove in a Palace car and collected a new background (Velvet Breughel) in Ealing en route. The Castle is vast and cold. The family now living around a courtyard in rooms built by George IV and with later Gothic additions. There was a van delivering coal at the entrance at which we should have arrived — so I was taken to the servants entrance and got a glimpse of the vast underworld of scullions — maids filling ancient looking water bottles and creating an almost medieval effect of bustle. A Sergeant telephoned for me to announce my arrival to the Lady in Waiting. He was well mannered and jocose — saying into the mouthpiece to some friend — Oh I didn't recognise your voice. I thought it was some gentleman speaking. At last we walked for miles along corridors to the Lady in Waiting's sitting room. A fire burning in the grate — Victorian chintz — A radio, an historical novel. The room was empty. More treks. The corridors have been stripped and most of the ornaments — Queen Mary's collection of miniatures — have been hidden from bombs. The corridors were icy. We passed rooms where the flowers are arranged — at this time of year there is nothing but chrysanthemums — masses of offices with leather boxes on the tables and the distant smell of a cigar. At last we found the Lady in Waiting trying to find me. Lady Hyde — in maroon wool — dowdy and nice. Just the right type. The Queen apologised there was no equerry to look after me. They were all out shooting with the King who would be back for luncheon. After enjoying the warmth of sherry we started to get the electric lights rigged up. It was a tremendous business and the equipment of wires and gadgets looked like a film studio. The State Rooms are magnificently ornate with tremendous doors — brocade on the walls and a wealth of gilt. There had been no fire lit in the grate since last year and the cold was arctic. I chose various rooms for the pictures and soon the Princesses appeared on the gothic landing I had elected for the pictures. They looked quite pretty in nondescript dresses — but there had been no time to plan anything specially nice for them and they did not seem to have had their hair freshly washed. However, they were very amiable and lasted through a long day's photography with tact, patience and even a certain gaiety. Princess Elizabeth has grown . . . when her face lights into a smile she is delightful. She has the same hesitance of speech as her mother — though when the Queen is present her daughter is most silent. We had not started to take pictures before the Queen walked out of her bedroom wearing a short tight banana coloured dress with a large cape of fox fur. She is an angel of tact and she made the day exceedingly pleasant. She seemed to think it great fun to photograph the Windsor gothic staircase and sauntered about the Rooms enjoying the occasion. She exudes a wonderful feeling of leisure and is never never hurried. I found it difficult to make unconventional groups of them — so often have they been photographed in formal attitudes that it is difficult to have a new approach on them — but an occasion like this brings down on me almost more conventionality than I am able to shake off. This gave me a feeling of frustration — otherwise I feel my day successful — The Royal Family behaved like any other kind and pleasant family.

The King was in a good mood . . . With him the Queen is miraculously clever — always handing him the stage — but saving the situation as soon as the Monarch has got into difficulties. Today the King appeared in loud tweeds — looking incongruous in these gilded rooms and since one is so accustomed to seeing him in uniform; during these days of war time. It had been a good mornings shooting and the King was ready for luncheon. Luncheon was ordered for 1.0. Then we'll take pictures afterwards. There was quite a party of people lined up in front of the fire. The French governess — Lady Hyde . . . then the new equerry, Wing Commander Pelly Fry who is doing this job as a rest from bombing. One or two other nondescripts including Gerald Kelly who has been in the household painting one bad picture after another for the last 4 years. Everyone groans at his continual presence but seem incapable of ousting him. When I mentioned that he painted complexions with such a leaden effect Princess Margaret said he wears his glasses all the time. The Royal Family reappeared . . . Deep curtsies and bows from the household. I found myself extremely un- nervous and talked in loud pitch to the Monarch about nothing in particular. We trooped into lunch. I was very proud to be placed on the Queen's right and delighted to find conversation so easy. She is dulcet — hesitant, amused and amusing, a most sympathetic combination. I feel that there is no one who could resist her charm once it were turned on him. Conversation is very 'polite and delicate' therefore one cannot launch on too controversial subjects. We discussed the rebuilding of London. The hideousness of much modern taste . . . the Duchess of Kent's talent as draughtsman and other such things. I was amused to see how some of the permanent courtiers behaved casually but with a surfeit of M'aming and Siring and yet Kelly kept his elbows on the table — blinked through his spectacles and aired his views . . .

At the end of the meal when the family filed out Kelly rushed back to finish his coffee and port. The meal was good. Macaroni, partridges in casserole and an apple white of egg flip dish. Refreshed I went back to the fray and only partially succeeded in getting the family into a good pattern. We took pictures in colour — and exposed altogether a great number of plates. Then Their Majesties had to go back to London. Perhaps I would do some more pictures in the summer — when they could wear prettier clothes — and perhaps the war — ? The Princesses rushed off to rehearse their Pantomime and I motored back to London in the blackout in the Royal van.

Family tragedy

The Duke of Kent was prevented from taking up his appointment as Governor-General of Australia by the outbreak of war. He was given instead a desk job at the Admiralty but disliked it and transferred to the Royal Air Force. There he was promoted to the rank of Air Commodore and later became Chief Welfare Officer. The Duchess became Commandant of the Women's Royal Naval Service (the Wrens). The couple left their home at Belgrave Square for their country house, Coppins in Buckinghamshire, where Beaton photographed them, together with their children, Prince Edward, Princess Alexandra and Prince Michael.

Beaton portrays the Kents as an ideal family, evoking the patriotic fervour of the period epitomized in plays such as Noël Coward's *This Happy Breed*. The Duke in his RAF uniform could have stepped straight from the film *The Way to the Stars*. Yet the truth was less happy. One of the Duchess's sisters was married to a German, the other to Prince Paul of Yugoslavia, who was forced to abdicate for allowing German war supplies through the country to Greece. The Duke did not greatly enjoy his war work, which consisted of a round of inspections of factories, shipyards and bomb damage. Then, on 25 August 1942, only seven weeks after the birth of his son Michael, the Duke took off for Iceland in a Sunderland flying-boat from the RAF base at Invergordon in Scotland. The plane, flying at the wrong height on the wrong course, crashed into the side of a mountain on the Caithness Estate of the Duke of Portland. The Duke's death left the Duchess bereft and his family financially unprovided for.

The return of romance

Beaton photographed Princesses Elizabeth and Margaret on 9 March 1945 but the resulting pictures were not released until February 1946. In the meantime peace had been declared. Beaton's choice of props and costumes revived the royalist idyll of 1939 which the years of conflict had so rudely shattered. He did not record the occasion in his diary, but in his *Photobiography* he recalls the sitting:

Before the sitting I was bidden to the Palace to see [Princess Elizabeth's] dresses, which were hung for display around the walls of her bedroom. Of all that we photographed that afternoon, by far the most successful was the pink spangled crinoline which was one of her mother's pre-war dresses, now altered to fit the daughter. These sunny, smiling photographs, taken against my old Fragonard background, had an enormous success, and were quite the most charming that I had yet seen of the Princess.

Princess Elizabeth's easy charm, like her mother's, does not carry across in her photographs, and each time one sees her one is delighted to find how much more serene, magnetic, and at the same time meltingly sympathetic, she is than one had imagined. In the photographs there is a certain heaviness which is not there in real life, and one misses, even in colour photographs, the effect of the dazzingly fresh complexion, the clear regard from the glass-blue eyes, and the gentle, all-pervading sweetness of her smile.

George VI in the uniform of Marshal of the Royal Air Force, at Buckingham Palace in October 1942.

1942: The Royal Family and Mrs Roosevelt

Beaton recorded the appearance of Buckingham Palace after the Blitz: on the left, buckets are set out in the State Apartments to catch rain coming through the bomb-damaged roof. In October 1942 Mrs Roosevelt was photographed with the King, Queen and Princesses Margaret and Elizabeth in the Bow Room of the Palace, its shelves empty of the royal Sèvres, which had been evacuated for safety.

'A group was made around the fire – a few suggestions from the King were soon overruled – now still – quiet – with which Madame President turned this way and that – her head high in the air . . . she shouted I haven't put a comb through my hair since New York, I haven't had any powder on my face since leaving Washington . . . Meanwhile the family smiled.'

The photographs of the Royal Family taken after the sitting with Mrs Roosevelt included several charming studies of Princesses Elizabeth and Margaret, then aged sixteen and twelve. They wear identical dresses as they often did in their early teens; these were pink with bows of blue pearls. The three portraits of Princess Elizabeth on the second row of this sheet of approved photographs were taken in the Bow Room of Buckingham Palace; Winterhalter's portrait of the Belgian Prince Leopold at the age of three months is framed into the wall above her. The single portrait of Princess Margaret bottom right was achieved by touching her sister out and painting in a left sleeve to the dress.

Overleaf: The Queen's plain wartime dress contrasts sharply with her rich costumes of 1939.

Windsor in wartime

These photographs, taken at Windsor Castle in November 1943, were released in the following April to mark Princess Elizabeth's eighteenth birthday. The King's uniform and the almost drab wartime outfits of the Queen and princesses look rather odd against the castle's florid Regency Gothic interiors. Nonetheless, Beaton achieved some remarkable portraits, such as this study (right) of the Queen and her daughters looking down from the landing of the Gothic staircase. As Beaton's diary account makes clear, the sitting was very cheerful — despite the freezing temperatures in the State Apartments — and even resulted in a royal joke (bottom right).

Family tragedy

The death of the Duke of Kent in a flying accident in August 1942 was the most serious personal affliction suffered by the Royal Family during the war. Beaton's wartime portraits of the Duke in his Royal Air Force uniform had transformed him into a glamorous hero.

At home, a month before his death, he posed with the Duchess and their two eldest children, Prince Edward and Princess Alexandra, whom Beaton also portrayed taking tea with their nanny. A year later the photographer returned to take this moving portrait of the bereaved Duchess (right).

The Return of Romance

As the war drew to its close, the weary public, tired of austerity and deprivation, hungered for images of hope. When Beaton was asked to photograph Princess Elizabeth in 1945 he at last felt able to revive the glamour and romance of his pre-war royal portraits. The photographs, taken in March, were released after peace in Europe had been declared. They caught the mood of the moment and were immensely popular.

In this portrait the Princess is wearing one of her mother's pre-war Hartnell crinolines. Beaton photographed her against both his favourite Fragonard backdrop and a curious winter scene (overleaf). The latter makes an unexpected setting for the flimsily clad princess but perhaps was intended to suggest that she was the harbinger of spring.

THREE

THE PAGEANT
1945—1960

THE MARRIAGE OF PRINCESS ELIZABETH TO PRINCE Philip in 1947 and the birth of their first children, Charles and Anne, brought a welcome note of optimism to the bleak postwar years. Then, in 1952, the early death of George VI and the accession of a beautiful young queen appeared to promise the dawn of a new and happier age. The Coronation of Elizabeth II in Westminster Abbey was an occasion of unforgettable pomp and theatrical spectacle, brilliantly evoked by Beaton's photographs. His royal portraits of this period re-create a vanished world. Even when his subject is the smiling, ever-popular Queen Mother or the occasionally nonconformist Princess Margaret he always managed to preserve the mystery of royalty. Youth was on the side of the Crown in the 1950s and never have its representatives appeared more magical and glamorous than in Beaton's photographs, where they act out their symbolic roles in the glittering pageant that served to lighten that grey era.

The Queen after the Coronation, 2 June 1953.
Seated in front of a backdrop depicting Henry VII's Chapel at Westminster Abbey,
she wears the Imperial State Crown and carries the orb and sceptre.

Although during the war the monarchy had suffered something of an eclipse, the course it took after 1945 was highly successful, if somewhat surprising. The gulf between it and society had dramatically widened: whereas before the war there had still been a relatively affluent aristocracy who lived on a scale not greatly smaller than that of the ruling house, matters were very different afterwards. Servants had virtually vanished and the great London houses, the settings for the grand events of the social season, were never reopened. Moreover, the postimperial age saw the decline of Britain as a world power.

This all suggested that the British monarchy would modernize itself as those in the Netherlands and Scandinavia had done, continuing the tradition of private domestic probity but abandoning the public grandeur of the prewar years. Instead the Royal Family was used to provide pageantry and spectacle for a nation still enduring years of stringent economy that persisted almost to the end of the 1950s. The marriage of Princess Elizabeth to Prince Philip, the Duke of Edinburgh, in Westminster Abbey on 20 November 1947 was the occasion of the first great postwar pageant. Although the Royal Family scrupulously observed the limitations of clothes rationing, the wedding dress by Hartnell was of heavy silk embroidered with ten thousand seed pearls from America. The King went into decline as a figure of public significance, as interest focused more on Princess Elizabeth and her burgeoning family. That interest reached its culmination in the Coronation in 1953, which elicited a huge surge of patriotic pride and fervent hopes for the country's future. It was a mood that was to be sustained more or less until 1960, the year of Princess Margaret's wedding, after which a very different era dawned.

A new generation

Beaton's *Photobiography* gives an amusing account of photographing the eighteen-month-old Prince Charles and newly-born Princess Anne in September 1950. The sitting took place at Clarence House, Princess Elizabeth's married home before her accession in 1953.

Sister Rowe warned me: 'You'd better hurry if you want to get her with her eyes open as she is already very sleepy.'

'Not a moment to be lost! Hurry, boys!' I instructed my assistants. We closed in upon the infant as she lay in Sister's arms by the window. But Sister sat with her back to the garden, keeping out most of the light from the baby who was already preparing to settle down for a comfortable afternoon's nap.

'This won't do!' Before we were able to readjust the scene, Princess Elizabeth, in a pistachio check dress, appeared, and she seemed very amused by the spectacle confronting her of so many grown-up people doing — apart from using their fingers — everything in their power to keep the baby's eyes open; bird-noises were made, shouts let off unexpectedly, hands clapped together, keys jangled. Three Rolleiflexes were suddenly put to great use, and another, filled with colour film, was at hand for a picture if the opportunity arose . . .

The infant Princess had lasted out a long series of disturbances extremely well, but now at last she became thoroughly exasperated. Prince Charles, too, was getting beyond control, and the volume of noise produced by the two children was quite ear-splitting. I was too tenacious, however, to be altogether lenient, and begged that we should be allowed to go down to the garden to take some pictures by the columns, through which the beds of salmon-pink geraniums and other vividly coloured flowers would make the sort of setting in which many people would like to see their Princess.

The scene in the garden became very chaotic, and at one moment I gave up any attempt at photography while I looked around. Prince Charles was rushing about the lawns wearing a policeman's helmet which he had found in the sentry's office; corgi dogs were barking and running in circles; my assistants were putting light meters up to one another's faces or against columns. Princess Elizabeth was looking about her in a mood of quiet amazement. I made one last attempt to organise another batch of pictures, and I felt that some of the mother holding her new-born against a background of the sunlit garden should be quite successful. But at last the time had come to call a halt. Prince Charles rushed to a waiting car to go off with a nurse for his too-long-delayed afternoon's jaunt, and Princess Anne sank into Nurse Rowe's arms for wonderful oblivion.

Queen Elizabeth the Queen Mother

Beaton photographed Queen Elizabeth (from 1952, the Queen Mother) on five occasions between 1948 and 1957. He deliberately returned to the image of her he had created in 1939: the Victorian age revived in the form of a gracious figure in a bespangled crinoline dress with an abundance of diamond jewellery, her very presence radiating light. Interestingly, the out-of-doors 'parasol' series of 1939 had no successors; instead Beaton used only grand architectural settings or painted back-cloths.

The first postwar sitting took place on 14 December 1948, the year of the King and Queen's Silver Wedding Anniversary. Despite the essential similarities, Beaton's interpretation of the Queen has changed over the nine years since he last photographed her alone. No longer is she a transparent fairy in white silk tulle; instead he has presented her as a strong and mature woman who might have stepped out of a nineteenth-century play. These were the years of Beaton's influential revival of Edwardian styles, beginning with his designs for John Gielgud's lavish production of *Lady Windermere's Fan* in 1945. Just as he dressed the strong female characters in a single colour which dominated the set, so in these pictures the Queen is attired in a black velvet crinoline by Hartnell with long black gloves, a costume made specially for this sitting. In several pictures she is photographed against a backdrop fairly closely based on the background of Winterhalter's famous portrait of the Empress Eugénie.

Very different in mood are the photographs Beaton took in May 1953. The 1948 sitting had been darkened by worries about the King's declining health; in 1953 the atmosphere was optimistic as the Coronation approached. In addition, barely a month before, Queen Mary had died, an event which consolidated Queen Elizabeth in her new role as Queen Mother, occupying the same position that Queen Mary had a generation earlier, the visible link between the historic past and the monarchy's future. She successfully combines an innate elegance and grandeur of bearing with an enormous warmth and animation of expression, in some pictures even bursting into a happy smile which still manages not to upset what is a formal state portrait. Beaton rightly describes her as having the quality of a 'great actress'. In these pictures the journey from a queen of romance to radiant royal grandmother is already complete.

The Coronation

George VI died on 6 February 1952. Sixteen months later, on 2 June 1953, Elizabeth II was crowned in Westminster Abbey. No coronation of any previous monarch had taken place with such a keen sense of universal participation in the sacred event itself. The presence of television and newsreel cameras, for the first time at such an occasion, increased enormously the emotional impact of a modest and vulnerable young woman pledging her life to her people. There was a political aspect to this: the newly-elected Conservative government was eager to re-assert the old order. One of its first acts had been to sweep away the 1951 Festival of Britain, whose theme was the promised utopia of postwar Socialism. A Coronation was an ideal opportunity for the reaffirmation of a hierarchical society which had in fact largely disappeared.

Princess Margaret, aged twenty-one, 1951. Overleaf: *Left, the Duke of Kent and his mother, the Duchess of Kent, in their coronation robes, 1953; right, the Queen and Prince Philip after the Coronation.* Pages 116–117: *Left, the Queen Mother, 1957; right, Princess Alexandra, 1953.* Pages 118–119: *Left, the Queen enthroned at Buckingham Palace, 1955; right, Princess Margaret, 1956.*

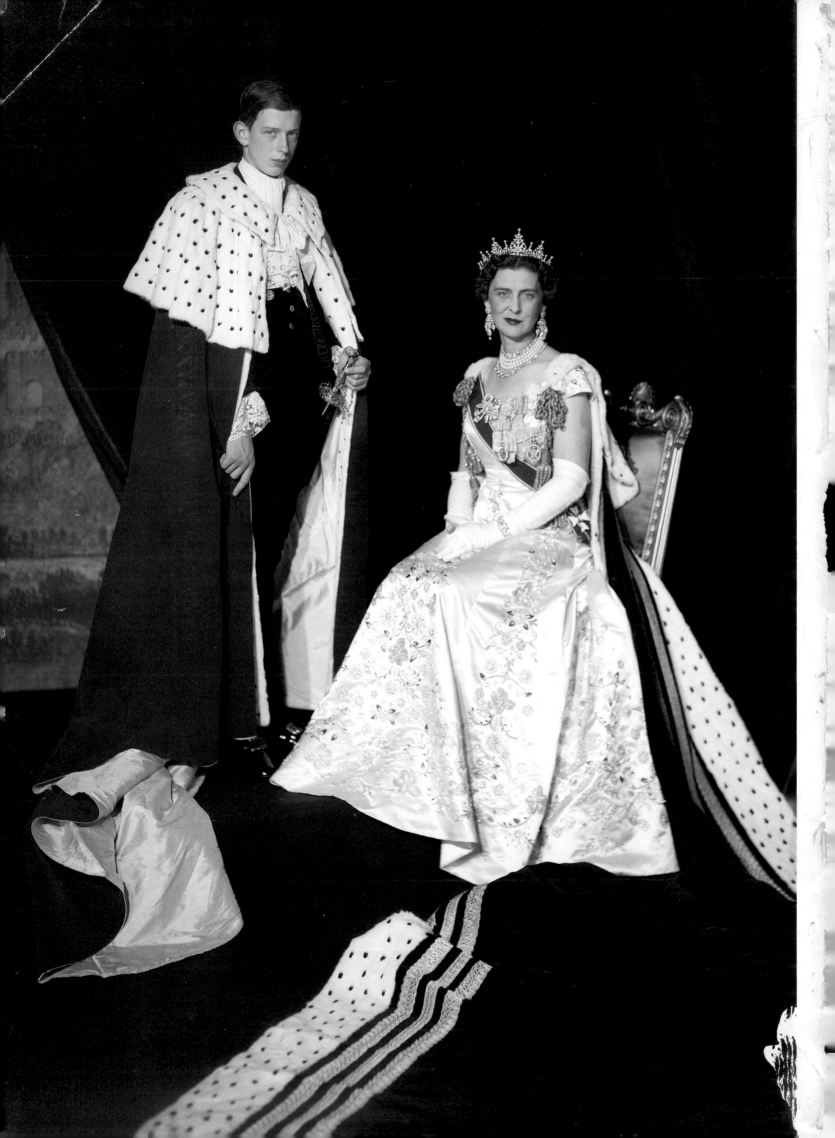

Beaton, with his innate visual and political conservatism, was the ideal man to interpret this event, but at the time he feared that a rival photographer, Baron, who was a friend of the Duke of Edinburgh, would win the commission. It seems that the choice of Beaton was due to the Queen Mother, who had sat so successfully for him in May. Beaton's diary account of the great occasion is very detailed. He was given a seat at the Abbey so that he could sketch the ceremony, after which it was time for the photographs:

I rushed off to the Palace and again had luck in completely avoiding the crowds — and after a few minutes was in the trade entrance being shown up to our familiar haven in the green drawing room. The others were there — Baba [Beaton's sister] wet through and cold was watching the return of the carriages — we stood on the balcony of the inner courtyard and watched the guards, the Kents carriage and the Gloucesters. Every window had the face of a skivy or flunkey at it and there was a group of a hundred household servants who raised a tremendous cheer as the Queen Mother came back waving and smiling as fresh as a daisy. Then to the sound of distant roars the wonderful bronze gold coach of the Queen with its Cipriano paintings and dark strawberry padded silk, bowled through the central arch and back to home. The Queen looked like a child in her tall crown and heavy ermine cloak and as she looked over her shoulder, she seemed utterly dazed and exhausted. It was not long before high girlish voices were heard at the end of the picture gallery. Oh Hullo, did you watch it — When did you get home? I peeped to see the Queen with her ladies, her excited children, the family leaning forward, asking questions, jokes, smiles, laughter. The high pitched voices of the Queen and Princess Margaret, the Duchess of Gloucester leaning forward — not a moment to lose — The Queen on her way to the throne room to be photographed by the Times. All sorts of Royalties popped their heads in on me and Prince Bernhard, then the Queen Mother proceeding towards me, her purple train being held aloft by her 4 pages and Prince Charles and Pss Anne who were running around to try to get a hold on it, and had eventually to have recourse to climbing under the purple velvet. The Queen Mother chuckling, laughing to show her dimples, her eyes as bright as any of her jewels, Princess Mgt. rather like a chorus girl with pink and white makeup — but neat and a twinkle in her eyes ... Quick! we started to take pictures. This way, that way, a certain shape was formed, a picture came to life, quick, quick. Then the Duke of Edinburgh put his face through a door — 'Margaret, you must come — you're keeping the whole group waiting'. Exit Margaret and Queen Mother ... Then the Queen came in with her ladies, cool, smiling, mistress of the situation — but tired — I suggested that she sit alone for some pictures by herself against my Abbey background. The lighting wasn't very good but no time to readjust — every minute of importance. Yes, I was banging away — getting pictures in the

---

Princess Alexandra in 1960, photographed in the garden at Kensington Palace.

can at a great rate, but I had only the foggiest notion of what I was doing — if taking black and white or colour. If giving the right exposure. The Queen looked very small under her robes and crown, her nose and hands rather pink — also her eyes somewhat tired. Yes in reply to my question, the crown does get rather heavy. One couldn't imagine that she had been wearing it now for nearly 3 hours. The Duke of E stood by making wry jokes ... He doesn't like me, would have preferred his friend Baron to take the snaps, and therefore was adopting a rather ragging attitude towards the proceedings. However, I tried in the few seconds at my disposal (like a vaudeville comedian establishing contact with his audience) to keep the situation light and mouvemente so that no one could settle down ... Like a juggler I moved the groups about — I took some of the Queen and the Duke and he had a grin on his face which ruined a few pictures but kept him in a good mood. Once I said in a cursory manner to the Queen what shall we do now? Will you go into the corner Ma'am? Go into the corner? She looked at me with wide eyes and a wide smile. No time for explanations. I took some of the Duke alone and they should be good — because he was nevertheless inspite of his preconceived notions about me, flattered by my attentions. He looked extremely handsome. Now to the other side of the room. The Queen and her ladies — Quickly, quickly, because this is just about the end. You must be tired Ma'am — yes — but this is the last thing we have to do — Now with the ladies in waiting — Can't we have the Duke? a slight alteration — You don't want me there do you — Oh yes — Oh no — well later. He went to get the Queen a glass of champagne. When they returned to watch the fly past (which we watched too from the inner balcony) Bill and my assistants drank the glass of the champagne which the Queen had only sipped — Back for more pictures — then the Gloucesters, but they were hurried off quickly for the Queen — again — only a few more of the Queen sitting at a table on which were my by now rather sad Etoile d'Hollande roses and clematis from Reddish — Now that's all. All over except the Kents ... mother nagging children, children nor mother ever still — oh my feet — oh I'm so tired — oh you moved Eddie ... You ruined that one Alexandra! ... Oh Oh Oh! — so that was all —

Princess Margaret

Beaton photographed Princess Margaret six times before her marriage in 1960: in 1949, 1951, 1954, 1955, 1956 and 1958. These were the years in which the young princess fell in love with a divorced courtier, Group Captain Peter Townsend, and was prevented from marrying him by the opposition of a family and establishment for whom the Abdication crisis was still a painful memory. The pictures taken on 8 July 1949 were for release on the princess's nineteenth birthday on 21 August:

She was at Lords for the Eton and Harrow match and got back a bit late, but she is such a *quick dresser that a few moments after her return she appeared changed into the new evening dress Hartnell had supplied her that morning — a dull dress of white tulle embroidered with sequin butterflies and a rainbow tulle scarf around the waist. She looked very pretty and wore quite a lot of make-up — and the eyes are of a piercing blue — catlike and fierce and so very pristine and youthful. There is no interim between a shut serious mouth and a flashing grin. No semi smile ... Her manner tremendously influenced by the Queen — not the hesitancy which Princess Elizabeth has caught but the high pitched rather strident cadence with the edge taken off by a kindness of heart which comes out in the voice towards the rather dwindling end of a sentence. This is very exciting she said as she walked up the long red carpeted arcade towards the Chinese drawing room in which we had placed all our complicated apparatus. I trust I haven't dragged you away from Lords — Oh it wasn't a drag, she said. She was amused by the whole procedure and I rather played up into her hands about the vague and general way I like my pictures and waiting impatiently the arrival of the boys with the metre reading or the raising of the tripod ... It is difficult to see in her features signs of her parents but the general appearance as she stood in her tulle dress, with soft demure hands, reminded me tremendously of the Queen, when I photographed her before the war ...*

The concentration needed during a photographic sitting is so great that it was difficult for me to talk — to have a conversation — so that the sitting was not in the nature of an interview — but I came away with the impression that she was amusing and witty (the light metre being placed near her was 'like having your pulse taken — This is my best side — the difference is quite astonishing' — and laughter about raising the head in order to shorten the effect of the nose) and kind and wishing to be helpful ... She had been up till 5.30 the night before (she likes the peace and anonymity of the 400 night club) and towards the end of the 2 hour sitting started to wilt and become very tired — but although she occasionally with a hopeless shrug and a delayed laugh, said no she couldn't raise an elbow — it was an impossibility — she was extremely patient and helpful and did the whole performance with a good deal of grace.

The new Queen

Beaton was summoned to photograph the Queen in November 1955, just before she went on a three-week tour of Nigeria.

It is difficult to find a new corner of the Palace for photographing. By now I have taken so many sittings here and have somewhat exploited all the possibilities. On closer scrutiny the rooms become very ugly and the quality of the furniture and decoration is quite vulgar. However we transported ourselves through long corridors through the Picture Gallery (where a middle aged 'page' with an anaemic face and a very bad cold was guarding the music room door beyond which Prince Charles and Princess Anne were having their dancing lesson (the white shoes and shetland shawl left outside on a banquette). We came to the Ballroom and I had the idea of taking the Queen sitting on one of the two enormous throne chairs placed under a vast crimson canopy. Martin [Charteris, the Queen's Private Secretary] was excited by the idea 'Just what we want for Nigeria'. But he wondered whether the Queen would be selfconscious about the plan 'If she can't sit in that throne who can?' What did I want her to wear? and what jewelry? Two full court evening dresses, the Malta Cross diadem made for George IV, and if possible the Garter Robes — complete with feathered hat — in fact three different changes. The courtiers and the young lady secretaries were still mooning about passing the time of day as I left — a message later to say that in principle the Queen had agreed to my suggestions — I was particularly pleased about the throne chair and the garter robes.

Beaton then returned to the Palace for the sitting itself:

I arrived exactly at 2.30 — and there were last minute readjustments to make, and every minute was occupied before the Page came in to herald the Queen just half an hour late. I hurried through the blue drawing room, and the music room to greet her in the yellow drawing room ... It had been a dull morning, and to spite the official weather reports, the afternoon had become duller. There was not only no sunlight filtering through the windows to give a lift to the scene, but there was an ugly foggy pall coming into the Palace rooms. The Queen brought no sunshine with her. The tulle dress she wore was of a cold ugly whiteness, unrelieved by the blue ribbon across her bosom. It was an uninspired, uninspiring dress that did nothing to aid the wearer — In the cold afternoon light the Queen looked cold. Her complexion extremely white — her hands somewhat pink. She did not look her best. I apologised for being the reason for her putting on court dress on such a cold afternoon. 'That's alright — but I miscalculated how long it takes'.

Grim with determination I conducted the Queen to the centre of a circle of blinding lights that had been placed in the blue drawing room ... No time for self-pity. I must go to do battle as quickly as possible. I looked in the ground glass of the big camera. Perhaps the scene would be more roseate here — but no, the same effect was created — the Queen stood looking very inanimate and it was for me now to keep her alert and amused — Luckily it seems that the Royal Family have only to get a glimpse of me for them to be convulsed with giggles. Long may that amusement continue for it helps enormously to keep the activities alive. Throughout the afternoon I found that it was very easy to reduce the Queen to a condition of almost ineradicable fou rire and thus prevented many of the pictures looking sullen and morose. We made lots of little jokes about 'Teeth' showing teeth for a second's exposure — showing teeth spontaneously ... This amuses me, and my amusement amuses the Queen.

A new generation

Princess Elizabeth and her first child, Prince Charles, born on 14 November 1948. 'I continued to snap, while Prince Charles exhibited a variety of happy moods. His mother sat by the cot and, holding his hand, watched his movements with curiosity, pride and amusement.'

Princess Anne was born on 15 August 1950 and was photographed with her mother a month later at Clarence House. The eighteen-month-old Prince Charles joined in, 'and at one moment — it reminded me of the great moment in The Sleeping Beauty ballet — he kissed the baby on her cheek and I was able to get the best picture of the afternoon'.

*Princess Elizabeth and Prince Charles at Clarence House in September 1950.
'Prince Charles was at the stage when he was interested in everything: a live
wire, he never flagged in energy, even when those around him were exhausted.
One minute he was up on a window-sill, giving an unexpected treat to the
passers-by below, pulling at the curtain cords; the next he was climbing on to the
sofa to take the cigarettes out of a silver box; then he would be absorbed with
interest in the working of his mother's snapshot camera.'*

Queen Elizabeth

These 1948 photographs are taken from the Queen's first major sitting since the romantic portraits at Buckingham Palace nine years before. Wearing the 'Indian' tiara, two diamond necklaces and her diamond tassel brooch, all brilliantly set off by Hartnell's specially made black velvet crinoline, she is posed to create pastiches of paintings by Winterhalter.

The Queen Mother

Five years later, George VI has died and Queen Elizabeth has found a new role as Queen Mother.

'At first I was somewhat despairing at not being able to arrange the curtains of my background to have any life or form. Suddenly all went well and the Queen Mum became very alive, alert, and amused. In fact it wouldn't have surprised me if I'd photographed her doing a wink ... My dear old Scottish maid Agnes on seeing the proofs sighed in rapt admiration, oh doesn't she look motherly! and indeed she does ... but she's so remarkable a personality with so much charm and intelligence and wit that everything becomes pleasant in her company. One feels life isn't difficult, that people couldn't be horrid, that everything is calm and serene.'

The Coronation

The most spectacular royal event of the twentieth century was also the climax of Beaton's career as royal photographer. The sight of a shy, beautiful young woman in the sumptuous regalia of an ancient monarchy was conveyed to the world largely through his photographs, taken at Buckingham Palace immediately after the ceremony in Westminster Abbey.

'The call from the Palace to say the Queen wanted me to do the Coronation photographs for posterity was such a relief as well as a joy and thrill. Another lease of life given me in my photographic career. "Would you please not tell anyone about it yet as when the news gets out so many people will ring up to know why they aren't being asked — and the Queen wants you". That night at a Ball I saw the young Queen and thanked her — "No, I'm very glad you're going to take them" she said, "but we'll be with circles down to here by then (she pointed halfway down her cheeks) then the crown comes right down to here (to the eyes) then the court train comes bundling up here and I'm out to here (sticks stomach out). There are layers upon layers — skirt and mantles and trains". She spoke like a young girl, full of high spirits and wonder — without any feeling of the weight of tradition ...'

The Queen and Prince Philip after the Coronation, 2 June 1953, in front of a backdrop depicting Westminster Abbey from the Thames. The Queen's dress, designed by Norman Hartnell, was embroidered with flowers symbolizing Great Britain and the Commonwealth. The Duke's uniform is that of an Admiral of the Fleet.

The elaborate equipment required for a royal sitting is revealed by this snapshot of Beaton taking his Coronation photographs of the Queen in the Green Drawing Room at Buckingham Palace (left). A selection from the pictures approved for publication is shown below. Prince Philip (right) disliked being photographed by Beaton and this was the only occasion on which he sat for him alone. His teasing made the task of taking group photographs all the more difficult. However, when he came to be photographed by himself, he was, wrote Beaton, 'flattered by my attentions'. He wears the stars of the orders of the Garter and the Thistle, together with the collar of the Garter.

CECIL BEATON PHOTOGRAPH

APPROVED PHOTOGRAPHS. SERIES B.647. 1953

B647·50   B647·52   B647·2   B647·5

B647·8   B647·3   B647·7   B647·114

'Then the return of the Queen Mother in rollicking spirits and slow voice "Do you really want to take a few more of me?" The children buzzing about her wouldn't keep still until she anchored them in her arms, put her head down to kiss Charles's hair and made an enchanting picture. This was really a good innings . . .'

The Queen Mother with her grandchildren, Prince Charles (left) and Princess Anne, after the Coronation. The Queen Mother wears a re-styling of the crown made for her own coronation in 1937, with the huge Koh-I-Noor diamond set into the front cross-pattée. The three-row festoon necklace of 105 diamonds was made at the instigation of George VI in 1950.

Princess Anne, then aged nearly three, caught by Beaton as she walks away from the Queen Mother
along her enormous velvet and ermine train. This sheet of contact prints (right) of the Duchess of Kent
and her family reveals the photographer's extraordinary ability to compose every shot into a picture.
One is of the entire family, four are of the Duchess's daughter, Princess Alexandra, and at bottom right
there is an exceptional portrait of her youngest son, Prince Michael.

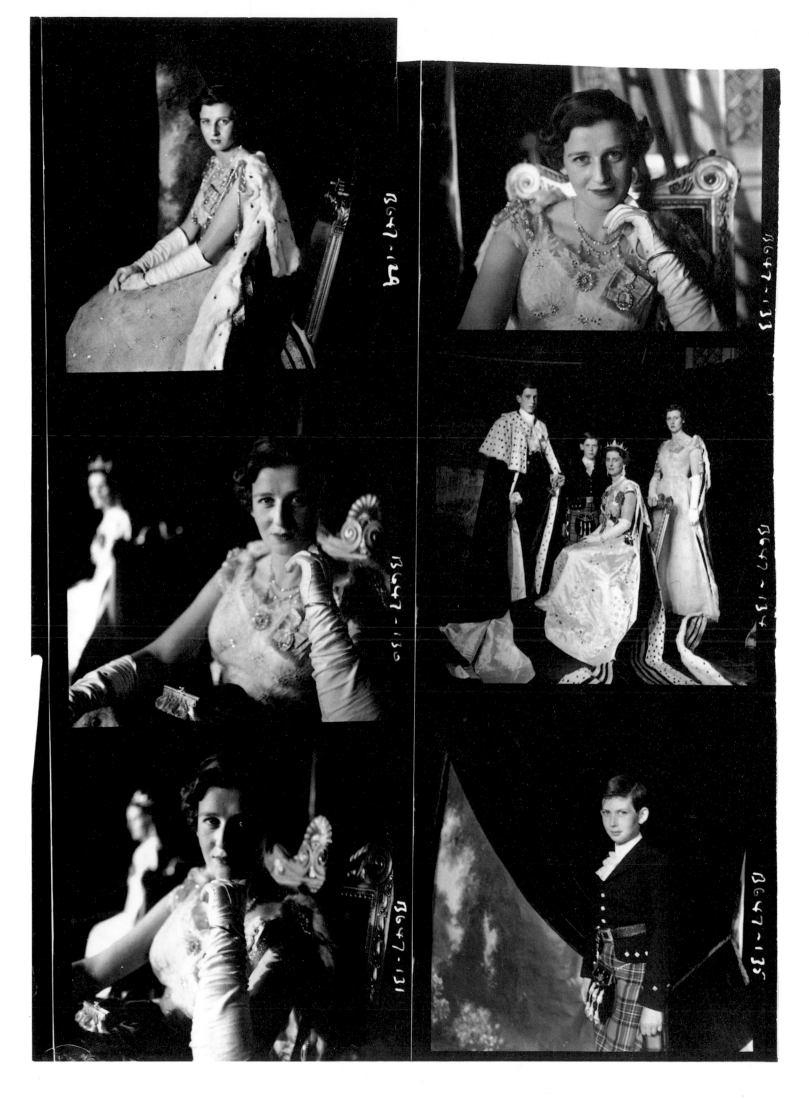

In his formal groups of the Royal Family Beaton evokes the traditions of state portraits. On the left (from top to bottom) are Princess Margaret and the Queen Mother, then the Gloucesters – Prince William, the Duchess, Prince Richard and the Duke. Beaton remembered how 'the Gloucesters came in with the two boys pulling their mother's train in every direction. The Duke, in his crown and shining complexion, looked like an Alice in Wonderland figure.' At the bottom is the Duchess of Kent with her children the Duke, Prince Michael, and Princess Alexandra, flanked by pages and ladies-in-waiting. On the right is the Queen Mother, resting her arm on a gilt Regency chair. Her ivory satin dress, like Princess Margaret's, Princess Alexandra's and the Duchess of Kent's, was designed by Hartnell.

A Victorian princess

Princess Marie Louise, a grand-daughter of Queen Victoria, was over eighty when Beaton photographed her in 1953. Her brief marriage to Prince Aribert of Anhalt was annulled in 1899 and thereafter she devoted herself to charitable works and the arts, especially music; she was also an intrepid traveller. When Beaton first photographed her, in 1949, he began by assuming that she must be 'an old gaga absurdity', but by the end of the session he thought her 'absolutely enchanting'.

Princess Margaret

'Princess Margaret is great news value. She is grown-up — an independent character showing more signs of interest in unconventional life than any member of the Royal Family since Edward Prince of Wales. She likes dressing up, flirtations, going to night clubs until all hours. Her "press" is rather scandalous. The American papers most anxious for any snippets they can get of her.' These twenty-first birthday pictures were taken at Buckingham Palace in 1951.

Beaton photographed Princess Margaret for both her nineteenth and twenty-first birthdays, in 1949 and 1951. The resulting portraits revealed to the world a new royal beauty. In 1949 he posed her against his painted backdrops (left and right) and remarked 'I was interested to see the change the last four years has brought about. The last time I photographed Princess Margaret she . . . two days later had her appendix snipped out. She wore homemade dresses – had lank hair – now she attempted a high degree of sophistication.'

In 1951 he photographed the Princess in front of the Louis XV tapestries in the West Gallery of Buckingham Palace (left and above). 'The Dior dress was a disappointment – colourless and indistinctive . . . but her complexion wonderful – and she had put on a wonderful array of make-up with vivid lips, rosy cheeks and black mascara . . . She has a tremendously alert brain – and is very quick in every way . . . Describing the embroidery on her dress she said I like it because it's got bits of potato peel on it.'

These relaxed studies of Princess Margaret with her Sealyham, Pippin, were taken in 1954 at Clarence House, where the Princess lived with her mother. The pictures combine Beaton's characteristic contre jour lighting with an informality of presentation that was to become increasingly important in his royal portraiture. Six of the contact prints (left) illustrate variant poses, each charming in itself.

Princess Margaret at Clarence House in 1958, photographed in front of her portrait by Pietro Annigoni (right). In the portrait above she wears part of a turquoise parure given to her mother by George V as a wedding gift.

'We started at once to take her against her Annigoni picture. This was a good send off. Easy to make interesting compositions and the reflected light of our lamps accentuated the dramatic effect and her likeness in the portrait looked like a Spiritualist's materialisation.'

The new Queen

These 1955 portraits were prompted by the Queen's forthcoming visit to Nigeria. 'The pictures in garter robes . . . should be good for now I knew how to arrange the lights, and to get the Queen three-quarter face with the head turned sufficiently back for the cheek bone to be clear and flattering. I was excited about the pictures taken in front of the Windsor Castle background.'

The Duchess of Gloucester and her sons

In 1953 Beaton went to Barnwell, the Gloucesters' sixteenth-century Northamptonshire home, to photograph Prince William and Prince Richard (left) with their mother. Just as he had them posed, one of the boys let off a gun which caused Beaton to jump with fright. Prince William (above) was then twelve and Prince Richard, the present Duke of Gloucester, nine. Prince William was killed in a flying accident in 1972.

The Duchess of Kent and her family

After the Duke of Kent's death in 1942, his widow made a slow return to public life. In this 1949 portrait she wears the same bow brooch and diamond earrings as in her 1937 sitting, together with a diamond fringe tiara given to her by the City of London on her wedding.

The Duchess's daughter, Princess Alexandra. This photograph was probably taken in July 1955, when the Princess was nineteen. This was one of the first occasions on which Beaton photographed her alone, just as she was beginning to assume a round of royal duties, at first in tandem with her mother.

The Duchess devoted herself to her private circle of friends from the arts and to her family, seen above in 1952 in the garden of Coppins, their country home in Buckinghamshire. Edward, Duke of Kent, was then aged seventeen; he is seen on the right with his ten-year-old brother, Prince Michael, below a portrait of their father.

Beaton found the most devoted royal sitter of his later years in Princess Alexandra. She became a new heroine, who not only bore the name of his adored Queen, her great-grandmother, but also combined her essential attributes, royalty and beauty. She is seen left in 1958 and above in 1959.

FOUR

THE TRANSFORMATION

1960–1979

THE 1950S AND 60S WITNESSED AN IMMENSE SHIFT IN THE image of the monarchy. The opposition to Princess Margaret's proposed marriage to Group Captain Townsend was only the most dramatic indication that the court was beginning to lose touch with the country. Slowly the Royal Family made a determined effort to swing away from stately pageantry towards a more relaxed and open appearance, and this is reflected in Beaton's delightfully intimate photographs of the Queen with her young children. The marriage of Princess Margaret to a commoner, the photographer Antony Armstrong-Jones, was hugely popular, for it marked an acceptance of the attitudes and way of life of the new generation of the 1960s. Beaton's final photographs of the Queen, taken in 1968, were yet another successful innovation. Their stark simplicity was in complete contrast to his royal portraits of previous decades, demonstrating that he, no less than the monarchy itself, had smoothly accomplished a major transformation.

Beaton's famous photographs of the Queen in an admiral's boat cloak, standing against a plain white background, were taken in 1968. They completed the transformation in his royal portraiture, away from fairytale romance, towards simplicity and directness.

THE DRAWN-OUT STORY OF PRINCESS MARGARET'S ILL-FATED love for Group Captain Townsend had taken place against a background of steadily increasing criticism of the Royal Family, culminating in 1957 when Lord Altrincham published an article attacking the monarchy's stuffy and outmoded image. Gradually the Royal Family began to adopt a more democratic way of life. For the first time the Queen's Christmas Day message to the Commonwealth was televised, the beginnings of a closer relationship with the medium that led to the celebrated 1969 TV documentary *Royal Family*, which unveiled to millions of viewers an edited version of the Windsors' private life, with a strong emphasis on its middle-class virtues.

After Princess Margaret's hugely popular wedding in 1960 pageantry largely went into abeyance for over a decade, with the exception of the notably relaxed and successful Investiture of the Prince of Wales at Caernarvon in 1969. In the 1960s ordinary life had a colour and a sense of spectacle which rendered the attractions of pomp and circumstance largely superfluous. It was the 'You've never had it so good' era of material prosperity. Not until after the recession of the 1970s had begun did pageantry re-assert itself with Princess Anne's wedding in 1973 and then the Queen's Silver Jubilee celebrations in 1977.

Beaton's working career by then was almost over, following his stroke in 1974, but it is interesting to speculate whether he would have responded to the new challenge, just as in the 1960s he rose successfully to the demands for informal, friendly images of royalty.

The birth of Prince Andrew

The Queen's third child was born at Buckingham Palace on 19 February 1960 and christened Andrew Albert Christian Edward. Beaton's account of this sitting is enormously tetchy.

The afternoon the pictures were to have been taken was brilliant and sunny — a postponement to the following day made things more difficult as daylight hardly existed. We were however set for action when my cheerful friend Sister Rowe arrived with the baby and the two young children. I was surprised and said 'Oh well I suppose we'd better start photographing right away if that would be alright'. Whereupon Princess Anne in a high fog horn voice said 'Well I don't know that it will be. I don't really think it will be' . . .

I had just started to organise a photograph when Martin nodded that the Queen was about to appear. To my surprise she was accompanied by Prince Philip who had just got out of a bed of 'flu. He looked pale and drawn. When I asked after his health he dismissed one unpleasant topic for another — the photographs — Well where do you want us? By now the new baby was enjoying a large bottle — all stood around stiffly while the baby sucked. I got very impatient and felt that the odds were ganging up against me. The Queen's face was real white — with not a trace of mascara on her lashes — her cheeks untouched by rouge and only a vague rubbing of lipstick on her mouth. Her dress of brilliant red — better than most of hers — was simple and without drapery. Will you sit there please — and the family around. They sat in the usual conventional poses — No good — I moved around — but the lights were arranged the other side of the screen for the Queen's pictures. I felt as if I were being chased in a nightmare when one's legs sink into the mire. The family stood to attention. I said something to make them smile so clicked. I clicked like mad at anything that seemed even passable. The baby, thank God, behaved itself and did not cry or spew. It sometimes opened its eyes. But even so I felt the odds tremendously against me. The weight of the palace crushed me. The opposition of this hearty naval type must be contended with, and due deference to the Queen. She seemed affable enough but showed no signs of real interest in anything . . . Not one word of conversation — only a little well bred amusement at the way I gave my instructions in a stream of asides — 'give me the ladder — Bring in the light here — give me the colour Rolleiflex!' P. Philip in that maddening Royal way kept suggesting I should use a ladder — take it from here — why not there — once I told him why not and quite firmly. Thank God he decided to take pictures himself — so with a camera that had a lens three times the size of mine he screwed up his eyes as he shot at his family. Do you mind my using your lights? I didn't feel I was taking any good pictures — nothing out of the ordinary. The baby was good. Sister Rowe was good — and I felt that the poor little Prince Charles was good . . . [He has] a perpetually hunched effect of the shoulders and a wrinkled forehead and pained look in the eyes as if awaiting a clout from behind, or for his father to tweak his ear or pull the tuft of hair at the crown of his head . . . I realised soon that he was nice and kind and sensitive — but that he has to be hearty — to be in a perpetual rugger scrum because that's what Papa expects of him. Somehow from his bright blue eyes — and sweet smile, I got more sympathy from him than from any of the others. Princess Anne continued her shrewishness — but almost unnoticed for I relegated her to the edges of the pictures and knew I could cut off her minny mouse feet in the finished pictures.

Perhaps I panicked — perhaps I should have taken more pictures with the remains of daylight — instead of having all floods turned on full. But I knew the lighting was dull — 'against life' — in that there was no natural source — no soft shadows. Yet I must not waste valuable time — for any moment the baby might scream — or the Queen be called away. As it was it was Prince Philip who called the whole thing off. As he loaded his camera anew he kept saying over his shoulder 'surely we've had enough — If he's not got what he wants by now he's an even worse photographer than I think he is!' Ha! Ha! that sort of joke is admirable for the Mess or an official review — but oh the boredom of today.

Princess Margaret marries Antony Armstrong-Jones

Princess Margaret married Antony Armstrong-Jones, later created Earl of Snowdon, on 6 May 1960. The wedding evoked a huge popular response, partly because the Princess's marriage to a commoner was seen to epitomize the new direction which the Royal Family had taken as it entered the 1960s. The event had special significance for Beaton as Armstrong-Jones was his chief rival as photographer of the Royal Family. His marriage temporarily eliminated him as competition.

After the couple had signed the Register I was taken ... in a police car and driven to the back entrance of the Palace. Here a long wait for the bride to return while I got more nervous and apprehensive as the clock defied our schedule.

The secretaries in the Press Room were drinking gin and eating potato chips as they watched the ceremony on television. Then at last the bride's coach came quietly into the inner courtyard while its occupants waved to the servants, all peering from ground floor windows. The newly marrieds came upstairs entering the green drawing room, the retinue of bridesmaids following quietly – a waste of time gossiping and drinking and receiving the first to return home – Then the ceremony on the Balcony – From where we stood on the far balcony we could see the Royal Family silhouetted waving to the cheering crowds below.

The Queen was enormously appealing to me. Her dress was quite wonderfully romantic – with a skirt of stiff folds – and everything of a kingfisher brilliance. She seemed calm and sweetly sad – and was most sympathetic even when being bossy and pointing a regal arm gave orders as to where each person should stand for the group.

Wonderful, at coming to my aid when photographs were becoming a chore, was the Queen Mother. She is so full of heart and understanding – and encouraged me to take informal pictures of the covey of bridesmaids – even when the others were impatient. The Duke of E put his head round the door – We want lunch. I happened to be very near the door and when he focused on the face next to his he got a shock and returned my grin with a grin. But he was very anxious to get the procedure over as soon as possible ...

The afternoon a nightmare rush seeing the proofs of the pictures to take some to the Queen Mother. She as irritated as I was by the stupidity of courtiers ... who thought the choice of pictures to give to Princess Margaret was more important than that of the Press. The Queen Mother tetchily said That's of no importance. They will have forgotten all about it in 2 weeks and this is for the dear public! She held the transparencies up against the

---

The Queen with Prince Andrew and the newly born Prince Edward, in the Blue Drawing Room at Buckingham Palace, 1964. Overleaf: Princess Margaret and the Queen, on the Princess's wedding day, 6 May 1960.

The Queen in the Blue Drawing Room, Buckingham Palace, 1968.

Prince Charles on one of the balconies overlooking the inner courtyard of Buckingham Palace, 1968.

A seventieth birthday picture of the Queen Mother at Royal Lodge in 1970.

Prince Andrew at the age of four, with the newly born Prince Edward, 1964.

curtain and said I hope the populace aren't too furious! She allowed me to choose the best. Inspite of rushing backwards and forwards until late at night my pictures were too late for most of the Press ... Nevertheless no hard feelings and a certain satisfaction followed the exhaustion.

The birth of Prince Edward

Prince Edward was born at Buckingham Palace on 10 March 1964. The sitting took place on 22 May. Although Beaton again, as in 1960 with Prince Andrew, felt 'weighed down with the difficulties', on the whole the sitting went extremely well, something which is borne out by the results. It is interesting to read about the enormous and spontaneous interest of Prince Andrew in the whole event, and to speculate as to Beaton's influence on his subsequent passion for photography.

I went to the Palace to make arrangements. The music room was again suggested. The dado rail cuts through every composition, decorations are obtrusive and the combination of blue colours and squashed strawberry brocade covered furniture is not a happy one. Best to be bold — eliminate the palace — concentrate on the Queen — on the child — that's really what is needed in any case ...

As we were leaving a lively scene of perambulators, children and dogs presented itself. The new born, trundled like a Georges de La Tour infant, was being brought in from the rain, Andrew was driving his tricycle in the hall, to be greeted with loving amusement by his girl eyed father. The Duke looked — inspite of the Cyclops effect and yellow complexion — at his most human. The children, with their nonchalent nannies and nurses, give the Palace the sense of reality that necessarily it lacks. I asked Andrew if he minded my taking photographs of him tomorrow. He smiled and said 'No I don't mind'. A welcome contrast to a reply I might have got from Pss Anne.

He returned to the Palace on the following day for the photography itself:

I waited in the picture gallery looking at some of the rather boring pictures, including a dull Vermeer. 'There he is' said the Queen in a loud little girl's voice — and Andrew ran towards me — Cheerful and polite and willing to please. At the end of the gallery ... was the Queen accompanied by her new born in the arms of the nurse. My heart lifted as I noticed the Queen was wearing rather a beautiful colour — a Thai silk dress — almost as light in tone as I would have wished ... The taste shown is of a safe, negative order, even the outsize diamond brooch she wore did not give a semblance of glamour. The mouth when

---

The Queen Mother at Royal Lodge, her home in Windsor Great Park; a seventieth birthday picture, 1970.

smiling is delightfully generous ... that was the saving feature of the photograph sitting: that mouth and Prince Andrew.

He is a boy with a quality that shines out with his niceness, and goodness and good spirits. He is trained to behave well, to be polite, and amenable — but he has the right instinct. Whatever test one puts him through he comes out well (May I take some more? or would you be bored? I'd like some more). From the moment the family group assembled themselves in our white oasis in front of the camera the pattern seemed to form and the lighting proved as luminous as we had hoped. Moreover the infant showed bonhomie and an interest in the activity that was going on. His adult behaviour pleased the Queen who was in a happy contented and calm mood — and not only smiled to my instructions but with amusement at the activities and fast developing character of the new born. Andrew was determined to be in every picture and behaved like a professional, adding the quality of charm of the too young to know really what it is all about. The design of the 3 figures improved each moment, and my enthusiasm shot like quicksilver to the top of the thermometer. I found myself rushing up and down a step ladder with the celerity of a mountain goat. The Queen remarked to Andrew on the speed with which I cranked the camera, he's much quicker than I am. I noted that sweat was running down my torso — the cause for such effort was justified. Sometimes I click with desperate speed hoping that some fluke would evolve. This time I felt that good results were being got immediately. The trio, from the ladder, looked appealing — luminous, vital and formed a good composition that was neither too unconventional nor formal.

The Queen's last sitting

The Queen last sat for Beaton in 1968. The photographs were taken largely with his retrospective exhibition at the National Portrait Gallery in view. That was the occasion of the unveiling of his portrait of the Queen in an admiral's boat cloak, a dramatic new image which received enormous coverage.

The Queen was in a good mood — or still had the remnants of a good mood on her for she gave off, to the crew — unaccustomed hoots of laughter followed by a giggle. She also has developed a manner of making quite a lot of faces — grimacing — and showing vitality ...

The Queen exhibited her first signs of amusement when I told her that I always tried to take photographs without enough light, that Geoff [Geoffrey Sawyer, his assistant] was always very against my instructions to turn out that light. Everyone looks better when there's less light I said rather tactlessly and followed this by telling Geoff to kill a vast standard.

She thought the whole procedure pretty strange — all rather odd and unexplicable. The ladders holding the blue background — the mess — the lights — but still she supposed it was alright. She'd do as requested. At first the effect of the lights was disaster. Nothing went right. I took pictures to cover up my frustration, each way she turned was worse than the last. The lights dead, we tried in quick succession the footlight on the floor — off — the dull light L. — off — Nothing came to light. Then suddenly she turned to the L. and the head tilted — and this was the clue to the whole sitting — the Tilt. I kept up a running conversation — trying to be funny — trying to keep the mouth light. She is averse to a big grin, does not like to be told to smile — but still is easily amused and I think feels that I am quite a cove — and is ready to laugh at me. By now I felt I had started to get something — and was busy duplicating this one pose that I felt had provided the afternoon's solution.

I asked the Queen to let me take some pictures in the mauve dress she wore underneath the cloak. This she was willing to do — I felt the streak of sun coming through the blue drawing room window onto the blue sofas would make a very happy colour combination. After a few of these were taken came the interval for changing regalia and setting. All preconceived plans were out. The sun was now shining for the rest of the afternoon and I had the many assistants bring in our background from the dark cavern and rely on good glorious daylight. Everywhere had sparkling possibilities. The Queen reappeared in a vivid turquoise blue dress, the Garter mantle and Queen Mary's pearl and diamond looped tiara. She looked splendid and I felt elated at the possibilities ... we banged away with great gusto, gaiety and real happiness. I don't think the Queen was for one moment bored and she seemed to respond to my flattery and praises.

A difficult Duke

This is the only occasion on which the Duke of Gloucester sat for Beaton, apart from the Coronation. It was prompted by a visit he was to make to war cemeteries in Greece and Turkey in May 1961. Prince Henry, third son of George V and Queen Mary, was a soldier in the Hussars, by predilection a countryman and a sportsman with a love of riding and shooting. His most important public appointment was as Governor-General of Australia from 1945 to 1947. As a character he was totally alien to Beaton's sensibilities, as the account of the sitting demonstrates.

Although I was ready to leave the house in time there were unaccountably no taxis to be had in the neighbouring ranks ... [and] I was half an hour late before setting off.

The Gloucesters' footman was out in the road looking for my arrival. There was a wide eyed group of ADC, Lady in Waiting, electricians galore etc. in the dark panelled hall, the atmosphere very tense and the D. of Gloucester scrubbed and shining like an apple with brilliant but bleary blue eyes explaining somewhat lamely that he had altered the plans by telephoning to his doctor for an appointment and that he had forgotten about being photographed in uniform. Would I be quick and take some of him now as he was.

He makes great bones of every sentence he manages to spurt out and said I'd better be photographed alone to begin with as when last he was upstairs his wife was having trouble with her hair ... The Duke then glowered at the camera with wild, mad eyes, walrus moustache and his snout, the hairless head and hands shone in the camera lens. Nothing of interest to catch — and time was short and the lights would not go right. Would it be possible to show a little short cuff? No I don't think that's possible. I was sad to see how old this nice young prince has become. A feminine flutter from upstairs then with much clearing of the throat and twitching of the lips the little Duchess of G. appeared in a day dress, fur stole and large diamond bracelet. She is ... terribly ... shy to begin with, but her inhibition has been greatly enlarged by being married to this Royal Personage. He is not only difficult himself but is surrounded by the protocol and nonsense that makes it almost impossible to be on terms with life. The result is quite agonising ... Everything is made so jerky, staccato and every molehill is a mountain. The Entourage add to the nuisance. I took some perfectly boring pictures of the 2 together. The Duke staring wildly into the lens and whispering I can't hold my hands like this — such a silly position — this isn't comfortable — can't sit on a chest like this — Have only five minutes before I'm due at my Doctor. The Duchess pretty ... looked terribly worried — unnecessarily worried — it didn't really matter if the D. was photographed inspite of the ADC pretending that it was so important that Persia and Greece had new pictures for presentation and publicity. No the Duke was in one of his moods — and he must go to the Doctor and to hell with the uniforms — and yet his valet was ready waiting upstairs and could get the Duke into any of them in less than ten minutes! In bubble bowler hat, however the D. went off to the Doctor. Something for him to do. But he'd not be gone long — perhaps — perhaps — Ma'am we could — persuade His Royal Highness to put on one of the uniforms when he returned ...

Really the whole atmosphere was so unlike anything that is happening today — it was a hangover of Queen Mary (His desk with all the little toys on it was just like hers). It has nothing to do with Kennedy, the atom bomb ... Oh dear me. I came away longing to relate the morning's idiosyncracies to someone who could laugh with me ...

'The family stood to attention. I said something to make them smile so clicked.' Prince Charles, Prince Philip, the Queen holding Prince Andrew, and Princess Anne, 1960.

The photographs of the Queen with the month-old Prince Andrew were Beaton's first experiments with plain white backgrounds for his royal portraits. However, he was more pleased with the portrait of Prince Andrew by himself, surrounded by flowers (opposite), taken with the aid of the Prince's nurse after the Queen had left. This is the first time that it has been published, for much to Beaton's disappointment it was not approved by the Palace.

'Lying on a cushion embroidered with full blown roses, and subaqueous looking leaves the baby [was] surrounded by the speckled carnations, lilies of the valley and spring flowers that I had brought into the Palace. The baby looked like a Spanish Christ as it waved its strong little arms in a baby's hallucination and opened ... eyes to the skies. This was a real moment of fulfilment. The pictures would be the best I knew.'

The birth of Prince Andrew

Princess Margaret marries Antony Armstrong-Jones

After her troubles in the 1950s, Princess Margaret's wedding on 6 May 1960 was greeted with particular joy. Beaton was less pleased, because her husband, Antony Armstrong-Jones (later created the Earl of Snowdon), was a rival photographer. Nonetheless, he was anxious 'to take interesting compositions of the bride and groom', but was largely foiled by the Duke of Edinburgh. Bride and groom (and camera tripod) are caught below in the mirror doors of the Throne Room. The bride, seen right on a balcony overlooking the innner courtyard of Buckingham Palace, wears a dress by Hartnell and a deep diamond tiara.

The bride and groom are shown overleaf amid a large family group. Standing beside them are (left to right) The Duchess of Gloucester, the Countess of Rosse (Armstrong-Jones's mother), Prince Charles, the Queen, the Queen Mother, the Duchess of Kent and Princess Alexandra. On the back row are the Duke of Kent, the Princess Royal, Prince Michael of Kent, Queen Ingrid of Denmark, the Duke of Gloucester, Robert Gilliatt (the best man), Prince Philip, Prince William of Gloucester and the groom's father, R. O. L. Armstrong-Jones QC. Princess Anne is the third bridesmaid from the right.

The Snowdons at home

Princess Margaret and the Earl of Snowdon with their children, Viscount Linley, aged four, and Lady Sarah Armstrong-Jones, aged one. Beaton took these photographs in 1965, in the garden of Kensington Palace, the Snowdons' London home. Such spontaneous out-of-doors photographs were an innovation for royal sitters; they reflect precisely the Royal Family's turning away from pomp during the 1960s.

The birth of Prince Edward

The Queen, Prince Andrew and Prince Edward at Buckingham Palace in 1964.

'The Queen's wide grin dominated the picture and other felicitous elements were provided by Andrew's blue wistful little boy's eyes — and the infant's holding its own by being alert, curious and already a character … The minimum of gurgles, or sicky mouth … and each time I asked the Queen if she had had enough — was just willing to continue a little longer. It's twenty past and those poor dressmakers are waiting! Look his eyelashes are all tangled! She said admiring the latest addition to the family — It's most unfortunate that all my sons have such long eyelashes while my daughter hasn't any at all.'

The Queen's last sitting

Beaton's last photographs of the Queen, taken in 1968, are among his most memorable royal images. He was determined not to repeat his earlier pictures: 'Must rely on a plain white or blue background — and determine to be stark and clear and bold'. The portraits of the Queen dressed in an admiral's boat cloak were a complete break with the past and received enormous coverage.

'There have been so many pictures of the Queen in tiara, orders and crinoline that I felt I must try something different. I asked Martin [Charteris, the Queen's Private Secretary] if a deer stalker cloak would be suitable. No he didn't think so but what about an admiral's cloak? navy blue serge. That sounded great and when I saw the cape in his office, felt this would be an enormous asset — we have seen too many two piece suits with brooch and wristwatch — this would be a great solution. Do you think it would be possible? I can only ask, Martin answered. You know the way it is — I do.
Martin telephoned to say the Queen had agreed to wear the cloak — was rather giggly about the whole thing — and said it didn't matter what she wore underneath it . . .'

The Queen in her robes as Sovereign of the Order of the Garter. She wears the Russian diamond and pearl tiara that had belonged to the Grand Duchess Vladimir and was sold to Queen Mary in 1921.

Overleaf: A sheet of contact prints of the Queen in the admiral's cloak. Beaton had difficulties with the pose until 'suddenly she turned to the L. and the head tilted — and this was the clue to the whole sitting — the Tilt'.

Pages 196 and 197: The Queen on one of the balconies overlooking the inner courtyard of Buckingham Palace and (right) seated on one of the gilt Regency sofas in the Blue Drawing Room.

Prince Charles

These photographs were taken in 1968, shortly after the Queen's sitting. This was the only occasion on which the Prince of Wales sat to Beaton as an adult. He is seen here on a balcony overlooking Buckingham Palace's inner courtyard and (right) leaning on one of the mirror doors that lead to the White Drawing Room.

'The sitting with the P of Wales was dull in comparison to the recent one with his mother. I blame the lousy London climate more than the Prince who incidentally is a simple nice, cheerful adolescent of 19 years. He has "gentle regard" a disarming smile and the tip of his nose is definitely modelled like a Gainsborough ... his hair is long and that is a triumph of independence over the influence of his Father and others at court ... He seemed jolly, yet sensitive and rather a dreamer. He seemed to look around the rooms we were in as if seeing them for the first time. Sometimes I did not feel like interrupting his reveries.'

The Queen Mother's seventieth birthday

The Queen Mother was seventy on 4 August 1970. These birthday photographs were taken at Royal Lodge, her residence in Windsor Great Park.

'The day was unforgettable ... like a visit to India, with rhododendrons and azaleas like mountains, growing in great alley-ways among the well tended Windsor Park lawns. The Q.M. was her usual kind good self and funny – while posing among the azaleas she said "Gardening at Royal Lodge".'

The Windsors in old age

Beaton maintained his friendship with the Duke and Duchess of Windsor throughout the 1950s and
1960s. When he photographed them in 1960 he used the same stark manner that he had applied to the
Royal Family for the first time earlier that year. The Duke was then sixty-six and
the Duchess sixty-four.

Beaton saw the Windsors for the last time in 1970. He took no photographs on that occasion, but he published an account of his impressions:

'Amid the barking of pugs, the Duke of Windsor appeared. His walk with a stick makes him into an old man. He sat, legs spread, and talked and laughed with greater ease than I have ever known. At last, after all these years, he called me by my Christian name and treated me as one of his old "cronies". He has less and less of these; in fact it is difficult for him to find someone to play golf with. The Duke still talks of his investiture as Prince of Wales, and asked me to find out where the crown is that he wore at Caernarvon.'

These contact prints, marked up by the photographer, are Beaton's last portraits of the Duke of Windsor, taken in 1960.

A difficult Duke

'While downstairs sitting stiffly in front of a white paper background in the room the Duke of Windsor had redecorated in the 1920s Chinese manner, the Duchess . . . heard the bowler hatted Duke returning from the doctor . . . The ADC followed the Duke up the staircase – came down glum – Nah Pooh. He asided to me perhaps if her RH were to ask his RH? I boldly faced the Duchess. Perhaps you'd try and prevail on the Duke to put on his uniform.

A pregnant silence. Electricians assistants – staff all stood in frenzied anxiety – ner – ner – yairs. The Duchess slowly rose to her feet . . . and . . . mounted the stairs. As I watched the progress in this deathly silence . . . the Duchess disappeared – in silence she reappeared . . . Not a word thrown from the banisters. We stood waiting in appalling silence. The Duchess was back in front of the camera before she answered my "any luck?" Ner – ner – no – I'm afraid he's rather tired after the Doctor – you know I s'pose he had to take his clothes off and put them on again – and he's rather tired.'

The Duke and Duchess of Gloucester, photographed at St James's Palace in 1961. Beaton appears in the mirrored door below. His diaries give a comic account of this awkward sitting, which seemed like a throw-back to an earlier age of stuffy protocol.

The marriage of the Duke and Duchess of Kent

The Duke of Kent married Katharine Worsley in York Minster on 8 June 1961 and the reception was held at the bride's family home, Hovingham Hall, where the photographs were taken. This was one of Beaton's unhappiest royal assignments. Forced to take pictures of the bride and groom amid groups 'arranged like drummers in a row' he 'had to shout to take one or two pictures of them alone together'. However, when he saw the photograph of the bride below, he recognized that 'under impossible conditions . . . one beautiful picture had been taken — a very nice rather ordinary girl, with an unusual strength of character had become a Cinderella Princess.' The Duchess's wedding dress was designed by John Cavanagh; the Duke wears the uniform of the Royal Scots Greys.

The Duchess of Kent with her pageboy and bridesmaids, including William Worsley, Willa Worsley and Emily Briggs (above). Princess Anne looks out at the camera on the right. 'The bride herself, like an Italian or German primitive with her neat blonde head, tip tilted nose and forward lifted tiara and long swan neck, was a real star. She moved with a ballet dancer's ease and grace.'

Princess Alexandra and Angus Ogilvy

Princess Alexandra married the Hon. Angus Ogilvy, second son of the 12th Earl of Airlie, in Westminster Abbey on 24 April 1963. The double portrait on the right was taken on their engagement. They have two children, James, born in 1964, and Marina, named after Princess Alexandra's mother and born in 1966, when the photograph below was taken. The family are in the grounds of their home, Thatched House Lodge in Richmond Park. Angus Ogilvy elected not to share his wife's public life and has continued his career as a businessman. Beaton's photographs reflect the family's private status, but their idealized ordinariness is also typical of the new direction taken by the Royal Family in the 1960s.

The final years

The children of Princess Marina loyally supported Beaton to the very end of his career. The
photograph of Princess Alexandra on the right was taken in the drawing room at Thatched House
Lodge in April 1974; it was his last sitting before a stroke which seriously curtailed his professional
activities. His final royal sitting was in November 1979, only two months before his death (above). His
sitters were Prince and Princess Michael of Kent with their eldest child, Lord Frederick Windsor.

Overleaf: *The Queen in the Blue Drawing Room at Buckingham Palace, 1968.*

Envoi : The Queen Mother looks back

Beaton's retrospective exhibition at the National Portrait Gallery in 1968 included the fullest public display of his royal photographs that had yet appeared. It was also the occasion of the publication of his photograph of the Queen in an admiral's cloak. The exhibition was opened by the Queen Mother, who was shown around the displays by Beaton. Her tour became a journey through royal history as she paused, reflected and remembered. The first room was dominated by a Venetian window opening out on to a photograph of a sun-dappled vista. At that moment, the present stood face to face with the past as the Queen Mother looked back at herself across nearly thirty years to that sunny afternoon when she had worn that floating lace dress and carried that parasol in the grounds of Buckingham Palace on the eve of the war. Beneath the window on a table stood ranks of silver frames containing even more memories: Princess Marina in Greek national dress and a tiara in front of the 'Piranesi' background; the Queen as a Princess in the Bow Room; young Prince Michael and Princess Alexandra of Kent. Beaton noted the Queen Mother's comments in his diary:

A very charming and sympathetic tour. 'Oh, I remember that sitting (her own). It was really the end of an epoch ... Oh, and the frieze. Yes I remember that Hesse diadem. That's one of the best of Marina. She was beautiful up to the last. And look at Marie Louise – what a character!' Laugh. A careful look at the Windsors. 'They're so happy, and really a great deal of good came out of it. We have much to be thankful for.' I did not over-egg the pudding by saying, 'We have to thank them for you', but merely responded, 'We have much to thank them for.' ... Interest in the new picture of the Queen. 'Yes, she told me I'd be surprised by it. It's very different, she warned me.' 'Do you like it?' I asked. 'Yes, I do. It has great character! The Prince of Wales. How delightful – such a nice boy – I'm so glad you liked him.'

Five years before, Beaton had sent the Queen Mother his now rare volume entitled *Cecil Beaton: Royal Portraits.* In reply he received this letter: 'I find it very nostalgic looking through the pages. The years telescope, and I suddenly remembered what I felt like when I wore those pre-war garden party clothes – all those years ago. It is absolutely fascinating to look back and I feel that, as a family, we must be deeply grateful to you for producing us, as really quite nice and *real* people!' (Vickers, p. 442).

The Queen Mother's shrewd judgement is as valid today as it was then. The House of Windsor has indeed every reason to be eternally grateful for the great artist who 'produced' them as being forever both happy and glorious.

CECIL BEATON'S ROYAL PORTRAITS: A CHRONOLOGICAL LIST OF THE COMPLETE SITTINGS

The sitters' books are now in the possession of Sotheby's, London, together with the rest of Beaton's photographic archive (apart from his royal photographs, which are in the Victoria and Albert Museum, and the war photographs, which are in the Imperial War Museum). There is no list of sittings before 1940, and so, for the early period, dates or approximate dates have to be reached from other sources. Even after 1940 the sitters' books confusingly work chronologically in two separate series, sometimes giving the exact date but usually only the year and the month. Even then entries can be as cryptic as the single word 'Royal'. Occasionally there is an indication of location and always the number or numbers of the negatives. Beaton did not write an account of every royal sitting but where he did the sitting is marked with an asterisk in the list below.

1930		Princess Louise, Duchess of Argyll
Late 1932 and/or early 1933		Prince George (later the Duke of Kent)
1935		Lady Alice Montagu-Douglas-Scott (later the Duchess of Gloucester)
*1937	Spring	The Duke and Duchess of Kent
*	2 June	The wedding of the Duke and Duchess of Windsor
1938		Princess Marina, Duchess of Kent
*	April	The Duchess of Gloucester
*1939	July	The Duchess of Kent and her sister, Princess Paul of Yugoslavia
*1939	July	Queen Elizabeth
1941	December	The Duke of Kent
1942	4 March	Queen Elizabeth
	August	Prince Michael of Kent
*	24 October	The Royal Family and Mrs Roosevelt
1943	11 March	The Duchess of Kent
*	20 November	The Royal Family

1945	9 March	Princess Elizabeth and Princess Margaret
	15 November	King George VI and Queen Elizabeth
*1948	14 December	Queen Elizabeth, Princess Elizabeth and Prince Charles
*1949	11 June	Princess Margaret
*	June	The Duke and Duchess of Windsor
	July	Princess Marina, Duchess of Kent
	August	Princess Marina, Duchess of Kent
	Undated	Princess Marie Louise
?1950	24 June	Queen Elizabeth
*	15 September	Princess Elizabeth, Princess Anne and Prince Charles
*?1951	19 July	Princess Margaret
1952	June	Princess Marina, Duchess of Kent and Princess Alexandra
	24 September	Princess Marina, Duchess of Kent and her family
*1953	5 May	The Queen Mother
?	20 May	The Queen Mother

	21 May	The Duchess of Gloucester with Prince William and Prince Richard	*	June	The wedding of the Duke and Duchess of Kent
*	2 June	The Coronation	1962	September	The Duke and Duchess of Kent and the Earl of St Andrews
	Undated	Princess Marie Louise	1963	January	Princess Alexandra and the Hon. Angus Ogilvy
1954	2 July	Princess Margaret			
1955	31 January	Princess Alexandra	1964	April	Princess Alexandra and James Robert Bruce Ogilvy
	July	Princess Margaret			
	July	Princess Marina, Duchess of Kent and her family		May	Princess Marina, Duchess of Kent
*	November	The Queen			
1956	July	Princess Marina, Duchess of Kent	*	May	The Queen, Prince Edward and Prince Andrew
	July	Princess Margaret			
	July	The Queen Mother	*	June	Princess Marina, Duchess of Kent
	July	The Princess Royal			
	November	Princess Marina, Duchess of Kent	1965	July	Princess Margaret, Lord Snowdon and their family
1957	May	The Queen Mother	1966	August	Princess Alexandra, the Hon. Angus Ogilvy and their family
*1958	February	Princess Margaret			
	December	Princess Alexandra			
1959	April	Princess Alexandra and the Duke of Kent	1967	March	Princess Alexandra, the Hon. Angus Ogilvy and their family
*1960	March	The Royal Family			
*	May	The wedding of Princess Margaret and the Earl of Snowdon	*1968	October	The Queen
			*	October	Prince Charles
	May	Princess Alexandra	1969	May	Princess Alexandra
	June	Princess Alexandra	*1970	May	The Queen Mother
	December	The Duke and Duchess of Windsor	1971	January	Princess Alexandra
			1974	April	Princess Alexandra
*1961	1 March	The Duke of Kent	1979	November	Prince and Princess Michael of Kent and Lord Frederick Windsor
*	March	The Duke and Duchess of Gloucester			
	March	The Duke of Kent and Miss Katharine Worsley			

SELECT BIBLIOGRAPHY

Beaton, Cecil, *The Best of Beaton*, with an introduction by Truman Capote, London, 1968

British Photographers, London, 1944

Cuttings Books, in the Archive of Art and Design, Victoria and Albert Museum, London

The Happy Years 1944–1948, London, 1972 (published in the USA as *Memoirs of the 40s*, New York, 1972)

and Buckland, Gail, *The Magic Image, The Genius of Photography from 1839 to the Present Day*, London, 1975

The Parting Years 1963–1974, London, 1978

Photobiography, London and New York, 1951

The Restless Years 1955–1963, London, 1976

The Royal Photographs, Exhibition Catalogue, Victoria and Albert Museum, 1987

Royal Portraits, London, 1963

Scrapbook, London, 1937

The Strenuous Years 1948–1955, London, 1973

The Wandering Years 1922–1939, London, 1961

The Years Between 1939–1944, London, 1965

Bryan III, J., and Murphy, Charles J. V., *The Windsor Story*, London, 1979

Buckle, Richard (ed.), *Self Portrait with Friends. The Selected Diaries of Cecil Beaton 1926–1974*, London and New York, 1979

Burke's Guide to the Royal Family, London, 1973

Cannadine, David, 'The Context, Performance and Meaning of Ritual: The British Monarchy and the "Invention of Tradition", *c.* 1820–1977', in *The Invention of Tradition*, ed. Eric Hobsbawm and Terence Ranger, Cambridge, 1983

Culme, John, and Rayner, Nicholas, *The Jewels of the Duchess of Windsor*, London, 1987

Danziger, James, *Beaton*, London, 1930

Day, J. Wentworth, *H.R.H. Princess Marina, Duchess of Kent*, London, 1962

Field, Leslie, *The Queen's Jewels. The Personal Collection of Elizabeth II*, London, 1987

Frankland, Noble, *Prince Henry, Duke of Gloucester*, London, 1980

Gloucester, Princess Alice, Duchess of, *The Memoirs of Princess Alice, Duchess of Gloucester*, London, 1983

Hartnell, Norman, *Catalogue of the Exhibition*, Brighton Art Gallery and the Museum of Costume, Bath, 1985–6

Silver and Gold, London, 1955

Hussey, Christopher, *Clarence House*, London, 1949

King, Stella, *Princess Marina. Her Life and Times*, London, 1969

Lacey, Robert, *Majesty. Elizabeth II and the House of Windsor*, London, 1977

Longford, Elizabeth, *The Royal House of Windsor*, London, 1974

Mellor, David (ed.), *Cecil Beaton*, Exhibition Catalogue, Barbican Gallery, London, 1986

Menkes, Suzy, *The Royal Jewels*, London, 1985

The Windsor Style, London, 1987

Mortimer, Penelope, *Queen Elizabeth. A Life of The Queen Mother*, London, 1986

Murray-Brown, Jeremy (ed.), *The Monarchy and its Future*, London, 1969

Rogers, Malcolm, *Elizabeth II. Portraits of Sixty Years*, Exhibition Catalogue, National Portrait Gallery, London, 1986

Russell, John, (introduction), *Buckingham Palace*, London, 1968

Smith, H. Clifford, *Buckingham Palace*, London, 1931

Vickers, Hugo, *Cecil Beaton. The Authorised Biography*, London, 1985

Ziegler, Philip, *Crown and People*, London, 1978

ACKNOWLEDGMENTS

This book was to have been written jointly with Sir Cecil Beaton's secretary, Eileen Hose, to whom Beaton left his archive of royal photographs on his death in 1980. Sadly her death intervened before the project was under way and the result must inevitably be the poorer for the loss of all her many insights and memories. She bequeathed the archive to the Victoria and Albert Museum: the decision that it should go there and not to the National Portrait Gallery must have been in recognition of my own friendship with Beaton during the last fourteen years of his life and in remembrance also of the retrospective exhibition of his portrait photographs which I staged in 1968 and which caused such a stir at the time, certainly giving Beaton, then in his mid-sixties, an enormous lift and paving the way for his knighthood in 1972.

The book would certainly not have been possible without the enthusiastic co-operation of Beaton's official biographer, Hugo Vickers, who provided me with transcripts of the passages from Beaton's diaries describing the royal sittings. To both him and Lord Norwich, co-executors of Beaton's Estate, I am grateful for permission to quote extensively from those diaries, which are largely unpublished in their original form. I wish to thank also a number of others for their memories of working with or for Beaton: Lord Charteris of Amisfield, Private Secretary to the Queen during the period of the majority of the sittings, and Patrick Matthews and Martin Harrison, who assisted Beaton at royal sittings.

The archive of Beaton's royal photographs is enormous and includes many photographs that were not approved for publication at the time. If the sitter is still living, the reproduction of such photographs must be sanctioned by the relevant Royal Households. I am indeed fortunate to be able to reproduce many unpublished pictures (which include all the contact sheets) thanks to the generosity of members of the Royal Family. Her Majesty The Queen has graciously permitted the publication of the picture of Prince Andrew as a baby, which Beaton held in high esteem. I owe similar debts of gratitude to Her Majesty Queen Elizabeth The Queen Mother, Her Royal Highness Princess Margaret and Her Royal Highness Princess Michael of Kent. Mr Robert Janvrin and Mr John Haslam of the Buckingham Palace Press Office have been courteous and helpful at all times.

For their assistance in the making of this book I am grateful to my former colleagues in the Photographic Section of the Department of Designs, Prints and Drawings of the Victoria and Albert Museum, in particular Mark Haworth-Booth. I wish also to acknowledge the support of Jim Close, the Chief Administrative Officer. Finally, I would like to thank Tessa Ruthven for the typing of the text and Louise Corrigan for transcribing and typing the original manuscript diary entries.

Roy Strong
January 1988

SOURCES OF ILLUSTRATIONS

All the illustrations in this book are drawn from the archive of Cecil Beaton's royal photographs in the Victoria and Albert Museum, London, with the exception of those that appear on the following pages: 26 (all pictures) courtesy of Sotheby's, London; 27 (top left and bottom right) courtesy of Sotheby's, London; 27 (top right) National Portrait Gallery, London; 28 (bottom left) Worcester Art Museum, Worcester, Massachusetts; 29 (bottom) National Portrait Gallery, London; 30 (top) Dulwich College Gallery, London; 31 (top right) The Wallace Collection, London; 32 (bottom) National Portrait Gallery, London, reproduced by kind permission of H.I. Spottiswoode; 42 (top right and left) National Portrait Gallery, London; 42 (bottom) Howarth-Loomes Collection, by courtesy of the National Portrait Gallery, London; 43 The Wallace Collection, London; 56 courtesy of Sotheby's, London; 113 Camera Press Ltd, London; 115 Camera Press Ltd, London.

INDEX TO THE ROYAL PORTRAITS